A-Z WESTON-SU

CW00408907

REFERENCES

Motorway	M5
A Road	A370
B Road	B3140
Dual Carriageway	
One-way Street Traffic flow on A Roads is also indicated by a heavy line on the driver's left.	
Road Under Construction Opening dates are correct at the time of publication.	
Proposed Road	
Restricted Access	
Pedestrianized Road	
Track / Footpath	
Residential Walkway	
Railway	Level Crossing, Station, Tunnel
Built-up Area	STONE RD.
Beach	
Local Authority Boundary	
Posttown Boundary	
Postcode Boundary (within Posttown)	
Map Continuation	20

Car Park (selected)	P
Church or Chapel	†
Cycleway (selected)	
Fire Station	■
Hospital	H
House Numbers	13 8 3
Information Centre	i
National Grid Reference	340
Police Station	▲
Post Office	★
Safety Camera with Speed Limit Fixed cameras and long term road works cameras. Symbols do not indicate camera direction.	30
Toilet: without facilities for the Disabled with facilities for the Disabled	▽
Viewpoint	
Educational Establishment	
Hospital or Healthcare Building	
Industrial Building	
Leisure or Recreational Facility	
Place of Interest	
Public Building	
Shopping Centre or Market	
Other Selected Buildings	

SCALE

1:15,840
4 inches (10.16 cm) to 1 mile
6.31cm to 1 km

0 ¼ ½ Mile
0 250 500 750 1 Kilometre

A-Z Az AtoZ
registered trade marks of Geographers' A-Z Map Company Ltd

www.az.co.uk

EDITION 4 2015

Telephone: 01732 781000 (Enquiries & Trade Sales)
01732 783422 (Retail Sales)

KEY TO MAP PAGES

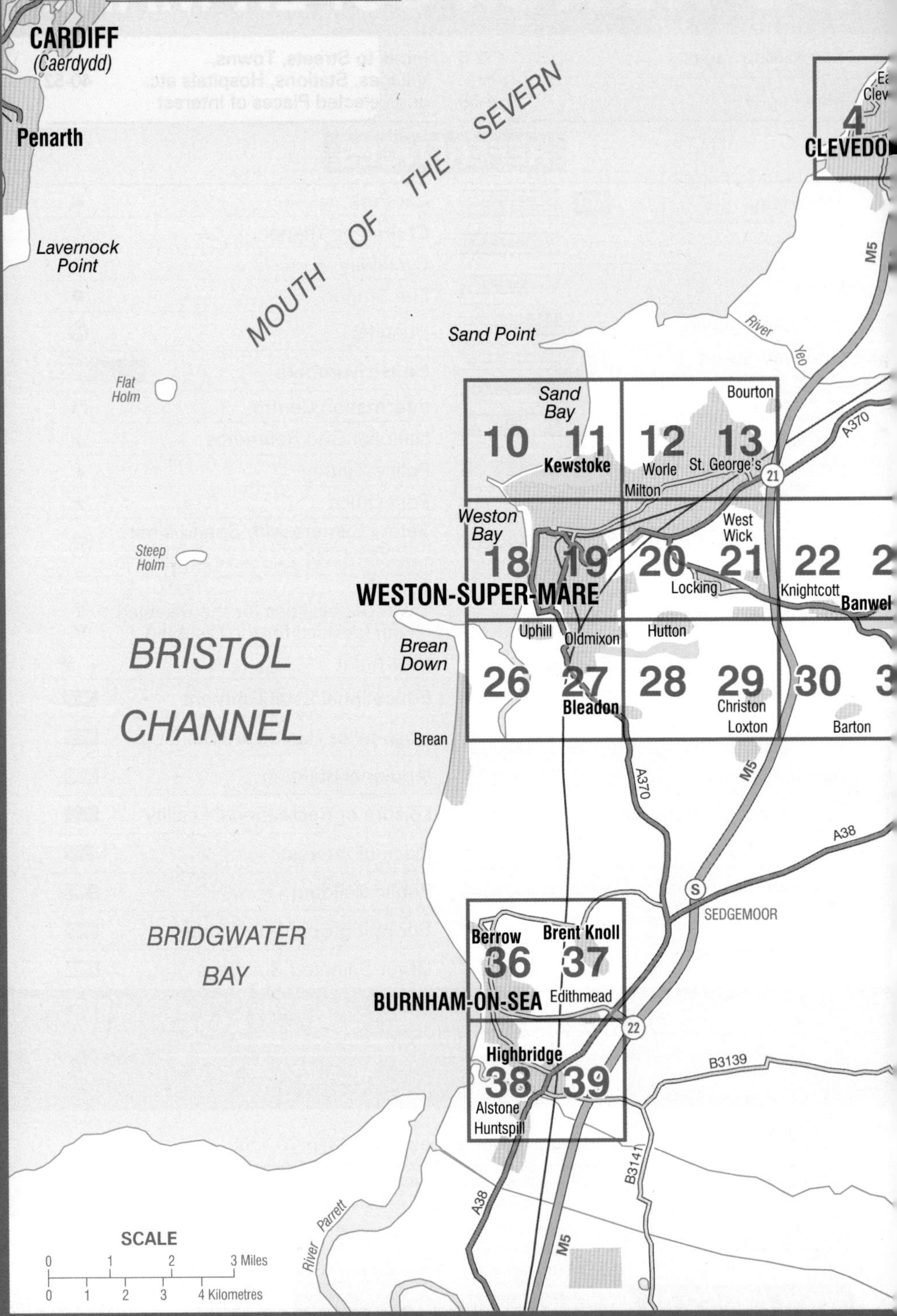

CARDIFF
(Caerdydd)
Penarth
Lavernock Point
MOUTH OF THE SEVERN
Flat Holm
Steep Holm
Sand Point
BRISTOL CHANNEL
BRIDGWATER BAY
4
CLEVEDO
Sand Bay
10
11
Kewstoke
12
Worle
13
St. George's
Bourton
Milton
Weston Bay
18
19
20
21
22
West Wick
Locking
Knightcott
Banwel
WESTON-SUPER-MARE
Uphill
Oldmixon
Hutton
Brean Down
26
27
28
29
30
Bleadon
Christon
Loxton
Barton
Brean
River Yeo
M5
A370
A38
21
S
SEDGEMOOR
Berrow
Brent Knoll
36
37
BURNHAM-ON-SEA
Edithmead
22
Highbridge
38
39
Alstone
Huntspill
B3139
B3141
River Parrett
SCALE
0 1 2 3 Miles
0 1 2 3 4 Kilometres

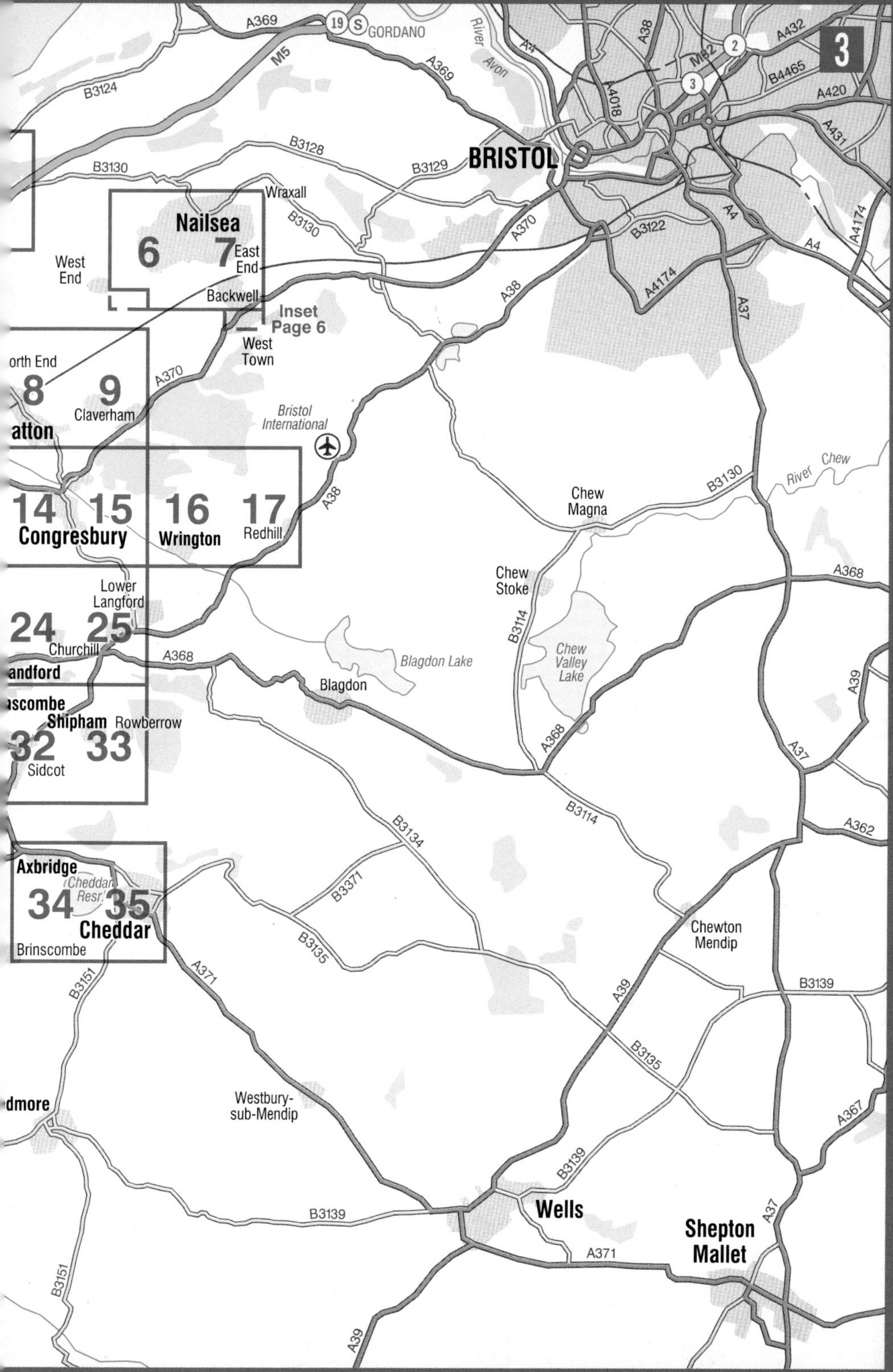
BRISTOL
A369
19
S
GORDANO
River Avon
M5
B3124
A4
A38
A4018
M32
2
3
A432
B4465
A420
A431
B3128
B3130
B3129
Wraxall
A370
B3122
A4174
A37
Nailsea
6
7
East End
West End
Backwell
Inset Page 6
West Town
orth End
8
9
Claverham
atton
Bristol International
14
15
16
17
Congresbury
Wrington
Redhill
Chew Magna
B3130
River Chew
Chew Stoke
B3114
Chew Valley Lake
Blagdon Lake
Blagdon
A368
Lower Langford
24
25
Churchill
andford
scombe
Shipham
Rowberrow
32
33
Sidcot
A39
A362
B3134
B3371
B3135
Axbridge
(Cheddar Resr.)
34
35
Cheddar
Brinscombe
B3151
A371
Chewton Mendip
B3139
A367
dmore
Westbury-sub-Mendip
Wells
Shepton Mallet

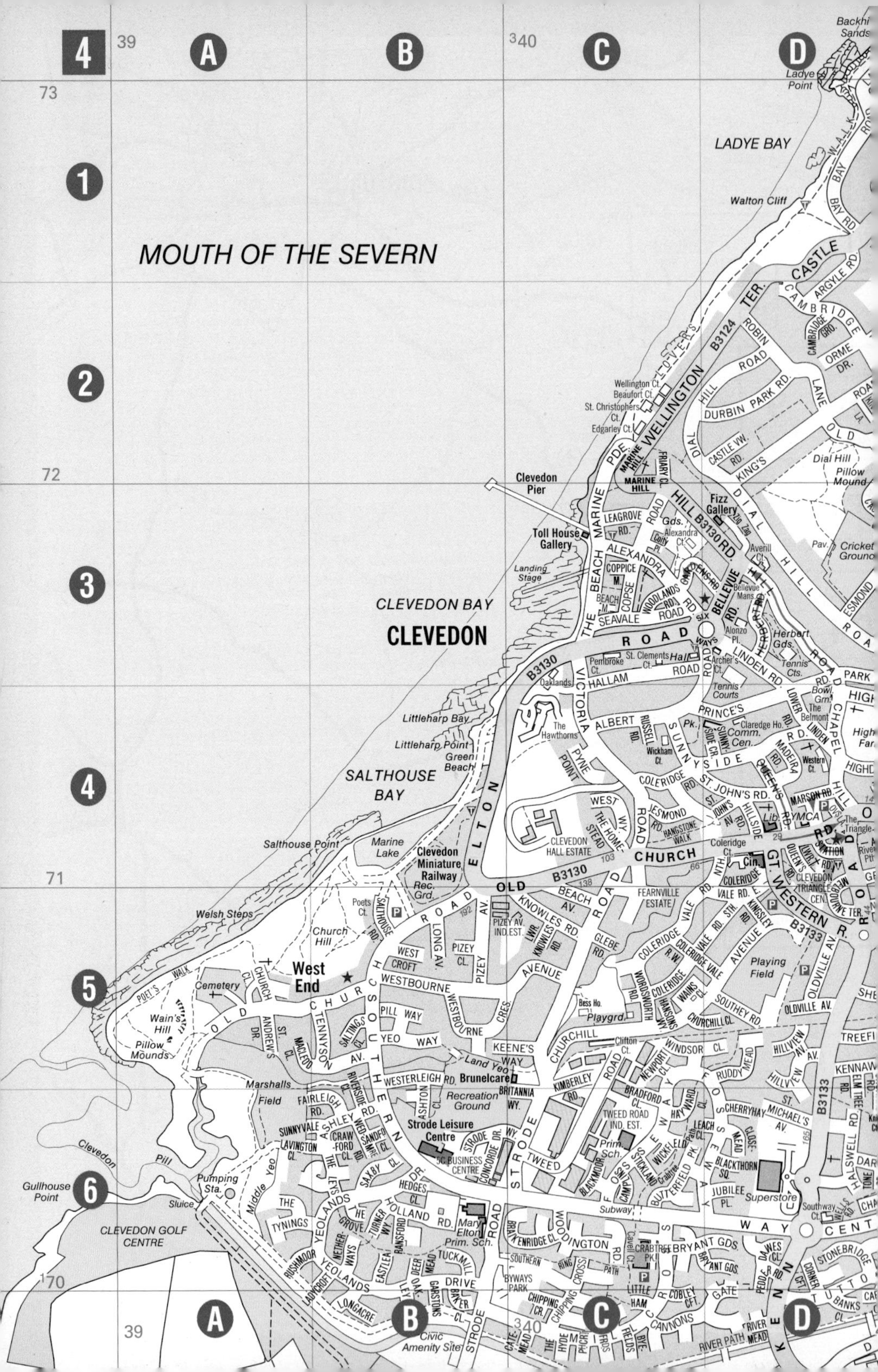

39
A
B
340
C
D
73
72
71
70
1
2
3
4
5
6
Backhill Sands
Ladye Point
LADYE BAY
Walton Cliff
MOUTH OF THE SEVERN
CASTLE RD.
ARGYLE RD.
CAMBRIDGE RD.
CAMBRIDGE GRO.
TER.
B3124
ROBIN RD.
ORME DR.
LANE
DURBIN PARK RD.
WELLINGTON
Wellington Ct.
Beaufort Ct.
St. Christophers Ct.
Edgarley Ct.
DIAL HILL
CASTLE VW. RD.
KING'S
OLD
Dial Hill
Pillow Mound
MARINE PDE.
MARINE HILL
FRIARY CL.
Clevedon Pier
HILL B3130 RD.
Fizz Gallery
Toll House Gallery
LEAGROVE RD.
Gds.
Alexandra Ct.
ALEXANDRA
Averill Ct.
Pav.
Cricket Ground
Landing Stage
THE BEACH
COPPICE M.
COPSE
BEACH M.
WOODLANDS RD.
GARDENS RD.
BELLEVUE RD.
Bellevue Mans.
ESMOND
CLEVEDON BAY
CLEVEDON
SEAVALE ROAD
SIX WAYS
Alonzo Pl.
Herbert Gds.
HERBERT RD.
ROAD
B3130
Pembroke Ct.
St. Clements Ct.
Hall
Archer's Ct.
LINDEN RD.
Tennis Cts.
PARK RD.
Oaklands
VICTORIA
HALLAM ROAD
Tennis Courts
Bowl. Grn.
HIGH
Littleharp Bay
The Hawthorns
ALBERT
RUSSELL RD.
PRINCE'S
Pk.
SIDE CR.
SUNNY
Claredge Ho.
Comm. Cen.
LOWER LINDEN
The Belmont
CHAPEL
Littleharp Point
Green Beach
PYNE POINT
Wickham Ct.
SUNNYSIDE
MADEIRA RD.
QUEEN'S
Western Ct.
HILL
SALTHOUSE BAY
ELTON
COLERIDGE RD.
ST. JOHN'S RD.
MARSON RD.
WEST WY.
THE HOMESTEAD
JESMOND RD.
HANGSTONE WALK
ST. JOHN'S AV.
HILLSIDE
Lib.
YMCA
The Triangle
Salthouse Point
Marine Lake
Clevedon Miniature Railway
CLEVEDON HALL ESTATE
CHURCH
Coleridge Ct.
Cin.
STATION RD.
Rec. Grd.
OLD
B3130
BEACH AV.
FEARNVILLE ESTATE
COLERIDGE
VALE RD.
NTH.
GT. WESTERN
CLEVEDON TRIANGLE CEN.
Welsh Steps
Poets Ct.
SALTHOUSE RD.
ROAD
LONG AV.
PIZEY AV. IND. EST.
KNOWLES RD.
LWR. KNOWLES RD.
GLEBE RD.
VALE RD. STH.
KINGSLEY RD.
B3133
Church Hill
WEST CROFT
PIZEY CL.
PIZEY
AVENUE
COLERIDGE VALE
R.W.
Playing Field
OLDVILLE AV.
West End
CEMETERY
CHURCH CL.
WESTBOURNE
WESTBOURNE CRES.
WORDSWORTH RD.
HANSONS WY.
WAINS CL.
SOUTHEY RD.
POET'S WALK
OLD CHURCH
Wain's Hill
ANDREW'S DR.
ST. CL.
TENNYSON AV.
SALTINGS CL.
PILL WAY
YEO WAY
SOUTHERN
Bess Ho.
Playgrd.
CHURCHILL CL.
CHURCHILL
Pillow Mounds
MACLEOD
KEENE'S WAY
Land Yeo
Clifton Ct.
WINDSOR CL.
HILLVIEW AV.
TREEFIELD
KENNAWAY
Marshalls Field
RIVERSIDE CL.
WESTERLEIGH RD.
Brunelcare
BRITANNIA WY.
KIMBERLEY RD.
NEWPORT CL.
RUDDYMEAD
FAIRLEIGH RD.
ASHTON CL.
Recreation Ground
BRADFORD CL.
HAYWARD CL.
CHERRYHAY
ST. MICHAEL'S AV.
B3133
ELM TREE RD.
SUNNYVALE
ASHLEY RD.
CRAWFORD CL.
SANDFORD RD.
Strode Leisure Centre
TWEED ROAD IND. EST.
LEACH CL.
MEAD CLOSE
HALSWELL RD.
Clevedon Pill
LAVINGTON CL.
THE LEYS
SAXBY CL.
STRODE DR.
CONCORDE DR.
SC BUSINESS CENTRE
STRODE WY.
TWEED
Prim. Sch.
BLACKMOOR
STICKLAND
WICKFIELD
BUTTERFIELD PK.
BLACKTHORN SQ.
Superstore
Gullhouse Point
Pumping Sta.
Middle Yeo
HEDGES CL.
JUBILEE PL.
Southway Ct.
Sluice
THE TYNINGS
YEOLANDS
THE GROVE
TURNER WY.
HOLLAND RD.
Mary Elton Prim. Sch.
ROAD
Subway
WAY
CENTRAL
CLEVEDON GOLF CENTRE
RUSHMOOR
NETHERWAYS
EASTLEA
RANSFORD
BRAKENRIDGE CL.
WOODINGTON RD.
Cavell Ct.
CRABTREE PK.
BRYANT GDS.
DAWES CL.
STONEBRIDGE
TUCKMILL
DEER MEAD
SOUTHERN
RING
CROSS
PATH
YEOLANDS
LADYCROFT
DRIVE
BYWAYS PARK
LITTLE HAM
COBLEY CFT.
PEDDER RD.
CORNER CFT.
TUTTON
BANKS CL.
LONGACRE
OAKLEY
GARSTONS
BAKER CL.
CHIPPING CR.
CHIPPING
GATE
CANNONS
RIVER MEAD
Civic Amenity Site
STRODE
CATEMEAD
THE HYDE
RIVER PATH
KENN

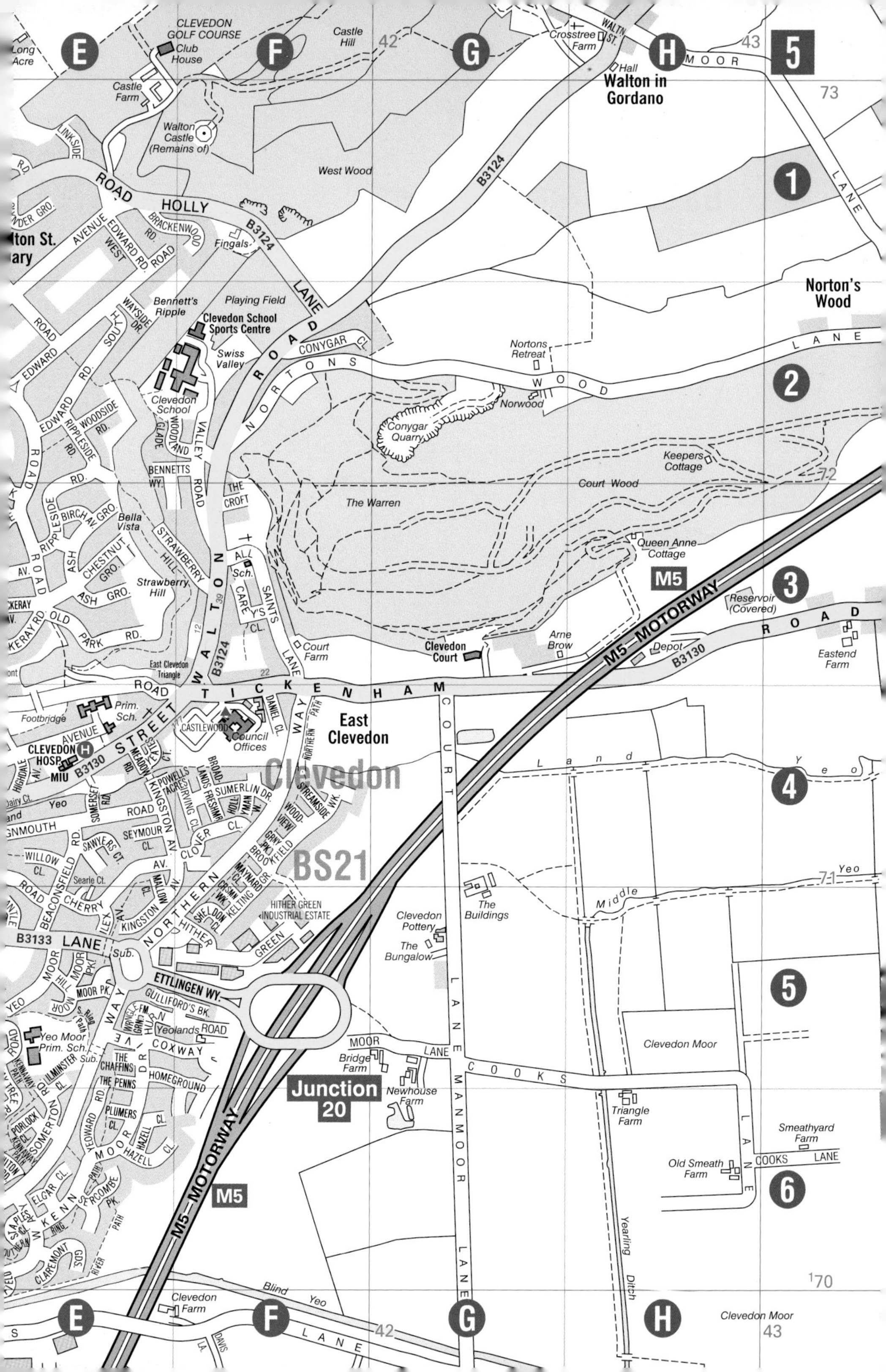
5
CLEVEDON GOLF COURSE
Club House
Castle Hill
Castle Farm
Walton Castle (Remains of)
Crosstree Farm
Hall
Walton in Gordano
MOOR
West Wood
B3124
HOLLY ROAD
LANE
Fingals
Bennett's Ripple
Playing Field
Clevedon School Sports Centre
Swiss Valley
Clevedon School
CONYGAR CL.
NORTONS WOOD LANE
Nortons Retreat
Norwood
Conygar Quarry
Norton's Wood
Keepers Cottage
Court Wood
The Warren
Queen Anne Cottage
M5
Reservoir (Covered)
M5 MOTORWAY
B3130 ROAD
Eastend Farm
Depot
Arne Brow
Clevedon Court
Court Farm
ALL SAINTS LANE
Sch.
CAREY'S CL.
THE CROFT
WALTON ROAD
STRAWBERRY HILL
Strawberry Hill
Bella Vista
BENNETTS WY.
WOODLAND GLADE
VALLEY ROAD
EDWARD RD.
RIPPLESIDE RD.
WOODSIDE RD.
BIRCH AV.
CHESTNUT GRO.
ASH GRO.
OLD PARK RD.
BRACKENWOOD RD.
WEST ROAD
WAYSIDE DR.
SOUTH RD.
LINKSIDE
East Clevedon Triangle
TICKENHAM ROAD
Prim. Sch.
Footbridge
CLEVEDON HOSP
MIU
B3130
STREET
AVENUE
CASTLEWOOD
Council Offices
DANIEL CL.
WAY
NORTHERN PATH
East Clevedon
Clevedon
COURT LANE
Land Yeo
BS21
KINGSTON AV.
MEADOW RD.
YEATES CT.
POWELLS ACRES
IRVING CL.
BROADLANDS
SUMERLIN DR.
FRESHMR
HOLLYMAN WK.
STREAMSIDE WK.
WOODVIEW
CLOVER CL.
BROOKFIELD
MAYNARD CL.
KELTING GR.
SHELDON CL.
SEYMOUR CL.
SAWYERS CT.
SOMERSET RD.
WILLOW CL.
BEACONSFIELD RD.
CHERRY AV.
Searle Ct.
ILEX AV.
MALLOW CL.
KINGSTON WY.
NORTHERN WAY
HITHER GREEN
HITHER GREEN INDUSTRIAL ESTATE
Dairy Ct.
Yeo
B3133 LANE
Sub.
ETTLINGEN WY.
MOOR HILL
MOOR PK.
GULLIFORD'S BK.
Yeolands ROAD
COXWAY
DRIVE
THE CHAFFINS
THE PENNS
HOMEGROUND
PLUMERS CL.
HAZELL CL.
YEOWARD RD.
Yeo Moor Prim. Sch.
ILMINSTER CL.
SOMERTON RD.
PORLOCK CL.
ELGAR CL.
CLAREMONT GDS.
RIVER PATH
Clevedon Pottery
The Bungalow
The Buildings
Middle Yeo
MOOR LANE
Bridge Farm
Newhouse Farm
Junction 20
COOKS LANE
Clevedon Moor
Triangle Farm
Smeathyard Farm
Old Smeath Farm
COOKS LANE
MANMOOR LANE
Yearling Ditch
Clevedon Farm
Blind Yeo
LANE
DAVIS LA.
Clevedon Moor
E F G H
1 2 3 4 5 6
42 43 73 72 71 70

6
A
B
C
D
1
2
3
4
5
6
Clevedon
BS21
Bristol
BS48
King's Hill
West End
West Town
BACKWELL
INSET
Chelvey
Tickenham Court
Tickenham Moor
Causeway Bridge
Heath Farm
Milton's Farm
Kingshill Church Sch.
Playing Field
Poplar Farm
Coombe Farm
Tower House Farm
Batch Farm
Nursebatch Farm
Battens Farm
Rugby Ground
Warehouses
Works
Warehouse
Depot
WEST END TRADING ESTATE
Hall
Grove Sports Centre
Grove Jun. Sch.
Hannah More Inf. Sch.
Young Wood Farm
Bizley House
Four Gables
Cherry Orchard
Nailsea Ford
Chelvey Court
Deerhurst Farm
Oldfield
MOOR LANE
DROVE
TICKENHAM
WASHING POUND LA.
WASHING CHURCH
CAUSEWAY
NORTH DROVE
Middle Yeo
Middle Rhyne
Land Yeo
Boundary
Tickenham
Ten Feet Rhyne
Brook
Parish
WATERY LANE
HANHAM WAY
PARISH BROOK RD.
RHYNE VW.
BRUNEL RD.
NORTH LA.
FIR LEAZE
BARNWOOD CT.
LEIGHWOOD DR.
NORTH LANE
ENGINE LANE
BLACKFRIARS ROAD
QUEEN'S WAY
HANNAH MORE ROAD
KINGSHILL POUND
KINGSMEAD
SILVER STREET
UNION ST.
CHAPEL LANE
ROCK AVENUE
ORCHARD
RIDGEWAY
TRINITY RD.
CHURCH LANE
OLD CHURCH RD.
WHITEOAK WAY
GROVE
UPLANDS
ST. MARY'S
THE CHIMES
KINGSTON WY
KINGSTON RD.
KINGSTON DR.
THE BRAMLEYS
NEWTON GRN.
WORCESTER GDNS.
BLAKENEY GRO.
ALLINGTON GDNS.
FERN GRO.
ST. MARY'S PK.
WHITESFIELD RD.
MOORFIELDS RD.
WAREHAM
HAZELBURY
ABBOTSBURY
LONG WOOD
NETHERTON WOOD LA.
CHELVEY ROAD
River
BREACH LANE
NAILSEA MOOR LA.
WEST END
MAIN RD.
WEST TOWN ROAD
A370
CHELVEY RD.
CHURCH LANE
RUSHMOOR
RUSHMOOR GRO.
MANOR CT.
THE GREEN
KELLWAYS
ROBINSON WY.
HILLSIDE
KAREN CL.
HILLDALE CLOSE
OAKLEIGH
CHANTREE CL.
ST. MARGARET'S CL.
LAWNSIDE
LOTTS AVE.
ST. ANDREW'S RD.
ST. JOHN'S RD.
SUMMERLANDS
DARK LANE
BRAMLEY DR.
Rec. Grd.
Football Gound
Tennis Courts
Bowl. Grn.
Pav.
PIT LA.
345
46
71
70
168
348
49

E
F
G
H
48
49
Jacklands
Playing Field
Hall
SOUTHFIELD ROAD TRADING ESTATE
BRISTOL ROAD
B3130
Wraxall House
Cradle Bridge
VINES IND. EST.
1
2
3
4
5
6
71
70
69
GREENFIELD
WOODLAND RD.
RIVERWAY
YEOMEAD
MEADOW
VALLEY WAY RD.
BIRDCOMBE CL.
MILTON CL.
CRESCENT
WOODLAND RD.
HEATH RD.
B3130 ROAD
SOUTHFIELD
TAVENERS WLK.
FRENCH CL.
THE WILLOWS
WITHY CL.
ROAD
WOODHILL VIEWS
STREET
LODGE
EASTWAY SQ.
HEATHFIELD RD.
FRIENDSHIP ROAD
HEATHFIELD WY.
CHAPEL CL.
STOCK WAY N.
HIGH STREET
WOODVIEW TER.
Superstore
Pegasus Ct.
STOCK WAY N.
THE COURTYARD
LINK RD.
Hobbs Ct.
BROCKWAY
STOCK
Clevedon Wk.
Somerset Sq.
CHRIST CHURCH CL.
Lib.
Coll.
Crown Glass Pl.
Scotch Horn Park
Scotch Horn Leisure Centre
STATION RD.
LAUREL DR.
SCOTCH HORN WY.
WINDSOR DR.
STATION
SCOTCH HORN CL.
WAY SOUTH
VALLEY GARDENS
ROAD
HILLCREST ROAD
HILL-CREST CL.
HILLCREST RD.
DUNKERY RD.
Nailsea School
Games Courts
Playing Field
HORWOOD RD.
NAILSEA PK.
PARK
NAILSEA PK. CL.
BEECH DR.
HOLLY CL.
CHESTNUT CHASE
THE HAMLET
MAYFLOWER GS.
OLD COTTAGE
BLACKTHORN WY.
BRIAR CL.
SCOTS PINE AV.
HAWTHORN
ASHVALE CL.
LARCH CL.
HAW-THORN WY.
SPINDLEBERRY GRO.
BIRCHDENE
CHESTERTON DR.
CAVERSHAM DR.
CERNEY GS.
COATES GR.
Golden Valley Prim. Sch.
Playing Fields
NAILSEA
OAKSEY GRO.
CHERINGTON
Pav.
Playing Field
TETBURY
TETBURY GDNS.
ROAD
NOWHERE LA.
St. Francis Catholic Prim. School
BIBURY
ADAMS CL.
BIRDLIP CL.
AVENING CL.
TRENDLEWOOD
WINCHCOMBE CL.
BUCKLANDS VW.
BUCKLANDS DR.
BUCKLANDS LA.
BUCKLANDS END
BUCKLANDS GRO.
Bucklands Batch
ELM LODGE RD.
YOWLES CL.
GREEN PASTURES RD.
SAWYERS CL.
CLARK CL.
RECTORY CL.
WARRY CL.
COOKS GDNS.
PASTURES
CEDAR
ROWAN CL.
THE OAKS
THE BIRCHES
TRENDLEWOOD WAY
CHURCH VW.
GREEN WATERCSS.
VALLEY WY.
Bell Pit Brow
YEO VIEW
SCHOOL
LANE
GLASTONBURY WY.
WELLS CL.
WIN-CANTON CL.
VYNES CL.
VYNES WAY
CREW
KERNE CL.
OAKHILL
HUNTLEY
SHERSTON CL.
SUNDLE CL.
SHETLAND WY.
CRICKLADE
GROVE RD.
BUDE CL.
CAIRN CL.
TURBURY AV.
ST. ANDREW'S CL.
HELSTON RD.
ST. AGNES CL.
ST. IVES CL.
TRURO RD.
CHELVEY RI.
FALMOUTH CL.
FOWEY CL.
AUSTELL CL.
East End
BACKWELL BOW
Brook Farm
COMMON
Dibden's Farm
Backwell Common
Old Farm
Schrubbets Farm
Cider House
Subway
Moorside Farm
Woolleys Farm
Playing Field
PORLOCK
HAYES
MAYFAIR AV.
ASH HAYES DR.
BERROW WY.
RICKFORD
CHARTERHOUSE CL.
RICHMOND GRN.
LITTLE MDW. END
WEDMORE RD.
FARLER'S END
CHARD CL.
QUEENS ROAD
BECKET'S LA.
BROOM FARM CL.
YOUNGWOOD LA.
AXBRIDGE CL.
WALNUT CL.
FOUR ACRES CL.
WOOKEY CL.
SHIPHAM CL.
CHEDDAR GR.
PERRINGS ROAD
MIZZYMEAD
Mizzymead Rec. Cen.
MENDIP CL.
POLDEN CL.
BRENDON GS.
HOLFORD CL.
DUNSTER GS.
White Oak House
YOUNGWOOD LANE
Coombe Grange
Youngwood House Farm
STATION CL.
Nailsea & Backwell
STATION ROAD
COMBESIDE
CHELSFIELD
LADYMEADE
THE CROFT RD.
WAVERLEY
FERNSIDE
ALISON GDNS.
AMBERLANDS CL.
THE AVENUE
BACKWELL
THE BRIARS
MOORFIELD RD.
WESTFIELD RD.
LONGTHORN
UNITY
MEAD
SLADES CT.
GARSTONS CL.
MARLE PITS
WESTFIELD DR.
WESTFIELD CL.
MARINERS DR.
MARINERS CL.
THE CRESCENT
WESTHAVEN CL.
MEADOW CL.
Tennis Courts
Backwell Leisure Centre
South Field Farm
Backwell School
A370
FARLEIGH ROAD
CADOGAN GR.
MOOR LANE
West Leigh Infant Sch.
RODNEY
EMBERCOURT DR.
MULBERRY CL.
RUSSETT CL.
Recreation Ground
ORCHARD RD.
Football Grd.
BRAMLEY DR.
WEST TOWN RD.
INSET
DARK LANE
ST. ANDREWS RD.
ST. JOHN'S RD.
BACKWELL
West Town
Bowl. Grn.
Tennis

42
43
A
B
C
D
68
67
66
65
1
2
3
4
5
6
Clevedon
BS21
BS49
Meadmoor
KENNMOOR ROAD
Barberry Farm
Say's Rhyne
LILYPOOL DROVE
Blackditch Rhyne
DECOYPOOL DROVE
EASTERN DROVE
CLAVERHAM
Little
Rhyne
Ham Farm
LANE
MOOR ROAD
Little River
HAM
NTH. END RD.
North End
NORTH END
Chestnut Farm
Horsecastle
B3133
Works
Rugby Football Ground
The Grange
Horsecastle Farm
Park Farm
Jone's Bridge
HAWTHORN CRES.
MEADOWLAND
GREGORY MEAD
MACQUARIE FARM CL.
DAIRY CL.
GRANGE FM. DR.
BRIAR MEAD
HORSECASTLE
Factory
WOODMILL
MOORSIDE
KENN MOOR
BRAMBLEWOOD
MARKET IND. EST.
SOUTH VIEW T.
JONES CL.
WAKEDEAN GDS.
FARM
THE WOOD KILNS
RD.
AVALON CL.
THE LAWNS
CL.
HORSECASTLE CRES.
WEMBERHAM
STATION RD.
HIGH
STA. APP.
LAUREL GDNS.
THE PARK
PARK
AV.
ATLAY CT.
BARBERRY FM. RD.
DURBAN WY.
THE AVENUE
STOWEY
Westmead
ARNOLD'S
BRUNEL WY.
Works
Factory
Osmond Bridge
Yatton
LAUREL TER.
ASHLEIGH CRES.
GRASSMERE RD.
ASHLEIGH RD.
MENDIP RD.
THE RIDGE
Gasholder
Works
WEMBERHAM
Stowey Rhyne
YATTON
CHERRY GRO.
CHERRY CL.
DYSONS CL.
THE EAGLES
HEATHGATE
ELBOROUGH AV.
MYRTLE GDNS.
PAGES CT.
SHINERS ELMS
WYCH CL.
GRACE CL.
LODGE CL.
DERHAM CL.
Derham Ct.
Yatton Jun. & Inf. Schs.
Lib.
PO
Bowl. Grn.
Sports Field
Hangstones Pavilion
Laurel Farm
Streamcross Farm
Rhyne
Branch
The Batch
Works
DERHAM
CLOSE
ROAD
CHURCH RD.
WELL LA.
BEECH RD.
BARNARD CL.
Hall
WESTAWAY PK.
STOWEY PK.
CLAVERHAM CL.
OLD FORGE
MARSH RD.
THE BATCH
ELM WLK.
WEST RD.
ELM
THE CAUSEWAY
Cross (Restored)
CHURCH CL.
CHURCH LA.
COURT AV.
RECTORY DR.
RECTORY
WAY
RD.
WESTAWAY CL.
STREET
FROST
HENLEY LODGE
HENLEY
Cricket Ground
Rectory Farm
MENDIP GDS.
MENDIP CL.
BIDDLE ST.
CHESCOMBE
BINHAY
LANE
ALEXANDER WY.
ROAD
Ten. Cts.
Sports Field
ROCK
HENLEY PARK
TRIPPS CNR.
BRAMLEY CL.
MENDIP
CADBURY FARM RD.
ROAD
B3133
THE FROST
Frost Hill
Cadbury Farm
14
Frost Hill
Hill Court
HILL
Coun Club
Westover Cottage
Rhyne

E
F
345
G
H
46
Midgell Farm
68
Kenn
River
River
Kenn Moor Gate
1
BS48
DROVE
Laurel Bank
Poultry Houses
Claverham Court
Home Farm
Walnut Bank
2
WAY
CLAVERHAM BROCKLEY
LOWER
JASMINE
South Bank Nurseries
LITTLEWOOD
67
LANE
Lower Farm
Grove Farm
Claverham Green Farm
Bristol
Lower Claverham
Chestnut Farm
Works
3
EAMCROSS
LANE
Riding Centre
The Rectory
LANE
Nursery
Cottage Farm
BROCKLEY WAY
HIGH ST.
Green Farm
MEETING
WITHYMEAD
Rose Farm
Manor Farm
DUNSTERS RD.
HIGH
FRANKLINS WY.
Works
Friends' Meeting House
LUKIN CL.
REAMCROSS
ANVIL RD.
4
ROAD
DR.
ORCHARD CT.
Orchard Chicken Farm
CHESTNUT AV.
BROADCROFT
BROADCROFT CL.
BISHOPS
Church Farm
Claverham Farm
HOUSE
Cleeve House Farm
CLAVERHAM
CHAPEL LA.
CLAVERHAM PK.
Prim. Sch.
Streamcross
Cleeve
66
LANE
HUNT'S
LANE
Nursery
Playground
Ten. Cts
Pavilion
Bishops Farm
BISHOPS MEAD
LANE
WHITEHOUSE RD.
GRAITNEY CL.
Playing Field
Cleeve Coombe
5
CLEEVE DR.
A370
Cleeve Court
HOLLOWMEAD CL.
WOODVIEW DR.
RD.
Hall
HOLLOW MEAD
ROAD
MILLIER
CLEEVE
Walnut Tree Farm
Cleeve Toot
MAIN
PLUNDER ST.
WARNER CL.
P
BLIND
HILL
CHAPEL LA.
Henley Farm
LANE
LA.
Yew Tree Farm
HILL
6
Goblin Coombe Farm
ROAD
RHODYATE
Henley Wood
Reservoir (covered)
WOOD LANE
Bickley
BLIND LA.
RHODYATE
65
Reservoir
15
Cadbury Hill
E
F
Reservoirs (Covered)
345
G
H
KING'S WOOD
46

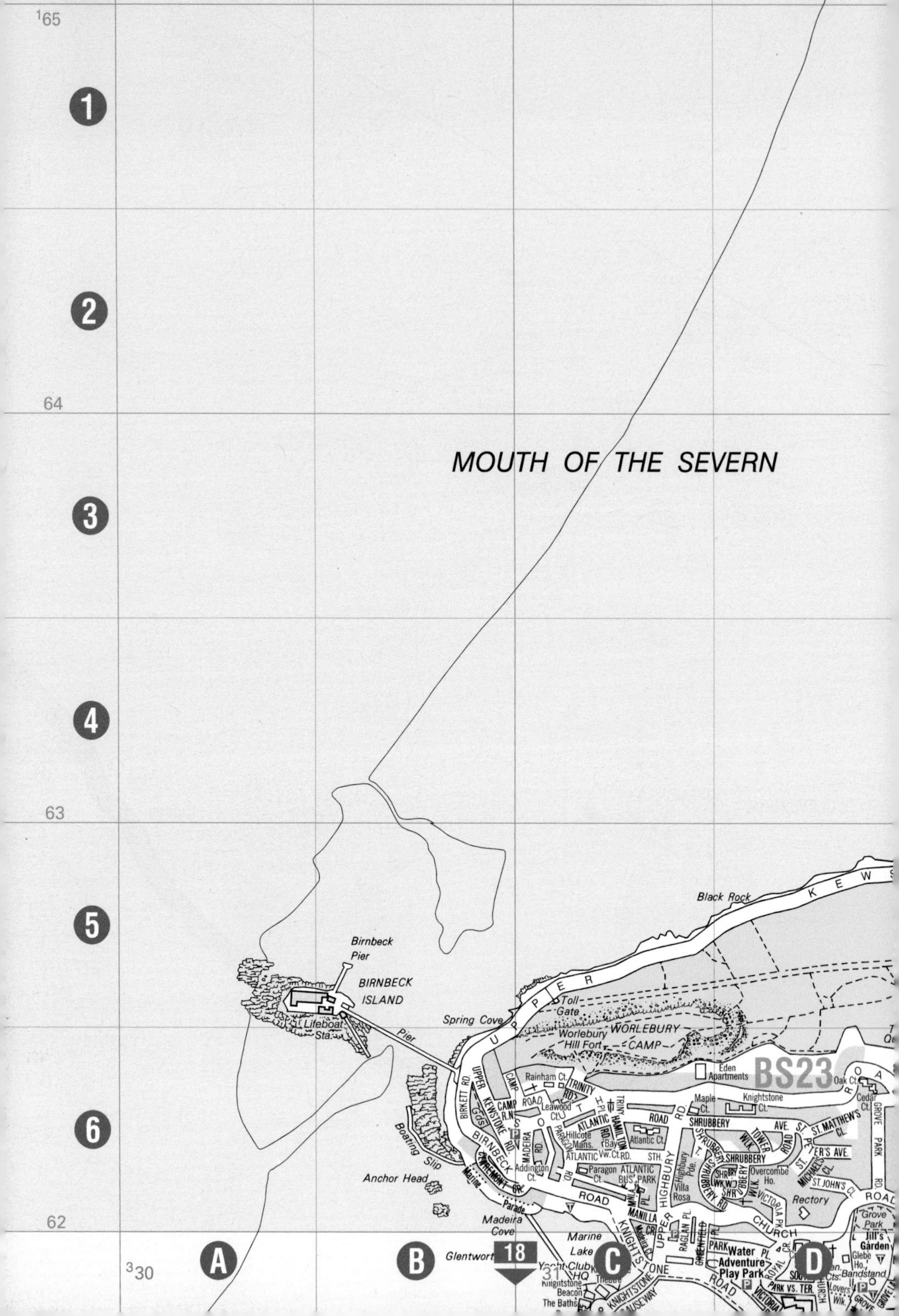

MOUTH OF THE SEVERN
Birnbeck Pier
BIRNBECK ISLAND
Lifeboat Sta.
Pier
Spring Cove
Black Rock
Toll Gate
Worlebury Hill Fort
WORLEBURY CAMP
Eden Apartments
BS23
Boating Slip
Anchor Head
Madeira Cove
Marine Parade
Glentworth
Marine Lake
Yacht Club HQ
Knightstone Beacon
The Baths
Theatre
KNIGHTSTONE CAUSEWAY
UPPER KEWSTOKE RD.
BIRKETT RD.
BIRNBECK
CLAREMONT CR.
CAMP ROAD
Rainham Ct.
TRINITY RD.
Leawood Ct.
MADEIRA RD.
Addington Ct.
Hillcote Mans.
ATLANTIC RD.
Paragon Ct.
ATLANTIC BUS. PARK
Atlantic Ct.
Bay Vw. Ct.
HAMILTON RD.
MANILLA PL.
Madeira Ct.
KNIGHTSTONE RD.
UPPER HIGHBURY RD.
Highbury Pde.
Villa Rosa
RAGLAN PL.
GREENFIELD PL.
Maple Ct.
Knightstone Ct.
SHRUBBERY ROAD
SHRUBBERY AVE.
SHRUBBERY WLK.
TOWER WLK.
VICTORIA PK.
Overcombe Ho.
Rectory
ST. MATTHEW'S CL.
ST. PETER'S AVE.
ST. MICHAEL'S CL.
ST. JOHN'S CL.
ST. PETER'S ROAD
CHURCH ROAD
Water Adventure Play Park
PARK PL.
ROYAL CR.
PARK VS. TER.
SOUTH CHURCH
Grove Park
Jill's Garden
Glebe Ho.
Bandstand
Lovers Wlk.
GROVE PARK RD.
Oak Ct.
Cedar Ct.
UPPER KEWSTOKE ROAD
18
A
B
C
D
1
2
3
4
5
6
330
31
165
64
63
62

E
F
33
G
H
34
SAND BAY
Sand Farm
SAND FARM LA.
MYRTLE TREE CR.
ST. BRIDGES CL.
SAND ROAD
BEACHLANDS PARK HOMES
COUNTRY VIEW CARAVAN PARK
SAND BAY HOLIDAY VILLAGE
COURT RD.
SANDBAY CARAVAN PARK
Kewstoke Rhine
BS22
STRATTON LA.
Nursery
Kewstoke
Rhyne
ELMSLEY LANE
NORTON ROAD
Weston-super-Mare
Home Farm
SOUTHSIDE CRES.
CROOKE'S LANE
BEACH ROAD
Hall
Rec. Grd.
ARDNAVE HOLIDAY PARK
THE AVENUE
LOWER KEWSIDE
KEWSTOKE
Cedarn Ct.
MANOR GDS.
ORCHARD CL.
Playgrd.
Vicarage
Kewstoke Primary School
KEWSTOKE CYGNET HOSPITAL
MONKS AVENUE
Monks Steps
KEWSTOKE ROAD
Toll Gate
WORLEBURY GOLF COURSE
WOODSPRING CRES.
Play. Fld.
Sch.
Milton Hill
Club House
WEST LINKS CL.
GREENACRE
WORLEBURY HILL ROAD
FAIRWAY CL.
THE RIDGEWAY
CLIFF ROAD
CLIFF RD.
FURZE RD.
PARK RD.
HILLCROFT
ST. DAVID'S CL.
PIMM'S LA.
HIGHLAND CL.
MILTON ROAD
THE CRESCENT
THE GLEN
MILBURY GDS.
CHALLOW DR.
PENRICE CL.
WORLEBURY HILL
Worlebury
WESTON WOODS
ASHBURY DRIVE
PRESCOT CL.
TURLEY WY.
NOTGROVE CL.
AYCOTE CL.
RENDCOMB CL.
MILTON BROW
VALDA RD.
FURLAND RD.
Milton
Ashcombe Wood
BRISTOL ROAD
HILLSIDE GDS.
CAVENERS CT.
GROVE DR.
ST JUDES
ROSLYN AV.
Jubilee
The Lodge
RINGWOOD GRO.
RANDEN CL.
ROCKINGHAM GRO.
PENDELSHAM GDS.
UNDERWOOD AV.
LEEWOOD RD.
EASTCOMBE GDS.
FOREST DRIVE
CRANBOURNE CHASE
Rockfield Cotts
FAIRFIELD CL.
Milton Prim.
CLARKSON AV.
Albany
Kingsholme Ct.
EASTFIELD PARK
LOWER UPPER
Tennis Courts
ASHCOMBE PARK
MILTON PARK
TICHBORNE RD.
KEW RD.
BRISTOL ROAD
MONTPELIER
TREWARTHA
BRENDON AV.
MANOR VALLEY
SNOWDON VALE
PENNINE GDNS.
SCAFELL CL.
ASHCOMBE PARK RD.
ASHCOMBE GDNS.
Pitch & Putt Course
Bowling Greens
Pav.
Tennis Courts
MILTON ROAD
Eastern Ho.
LANDEMANN CIRCUS
ARUNDELL
MONT PELIER
EAST
Lansdown Ct.
Rayneswood
Munscroft Ct.
Arundell Ct.
Landemann Path
Montpelier Path
SOUTHSIDE
CEMETERY
War Mem.
19
Woodside Ct.
HAZELDENE RD.
SEDGEMOOR RD.
DUMFRY
ASHLEIGH CL.
BELGRAVE RD.
WOODSTOCK RD.
SOMERDALE AV.
BATHURST RD.
EWART ROAD
RISE
62
63
64
65
Manscombe Farm
1
2
3
4
5
6
12
Playing

A
B
C
D
1
2
3
4
5
6
34
335
165
64
63
62
Rhyne
ELMSLEY LANE
Redcroft
FOSS LANE
COLLUM LANE
Northfield
Kewstoke
SAND ROAD
Nursery
ELMSLEY
NORTON
Norton Farm
Myrtle Farm
Norton Court Farm
Manor Farm
Greenway Farm
Weston-super-Mare Crematorium
Ebdon Rd. Cemetery
Weston-super-Mar
LOWER
Home Farm
Norton
NORTON LANE
LYEFIELD ROAD
KEWSTOKE
11
KEWSTOKE ROAD
Kewstoke Primary School
Worle Hill
GOLF COURSE
The Observatory
Works
WORLEBURY GOLF COURSE
Milton Hill
Club House
WORLEBURY HILL ROAD
Ranscombe Farm
Stonycroft
BS22
QUEEN'S ROAD
LOWER ROAD
KEWSTOKE ROAD
Harwood Grn.
Play. Fld.
FALLOWFIELD
St. Mark's Prim. Sch.
EBDON ROAD
St. Martins Ct.
HOLLOW LA.
WORLE CT.
LAWRENCE ROAD
Worle Village Prim. Sch.
Lib.
Knightstone Pl.
WORLE
STATION ROAD
Fussells Court
Rec. Grd.
Lewis Court
Westonia
Canon's Wlk.
St. Martin's C of E Prim. Sch.
CHURCH ROAD
SPRING HILL
HIGH STREET
BALMORAL WAY
PLESHEY CL.
Milton
BRISTOL ROAD
Jubilee Path
Milton Park Prim. Sch.
MILTON PARK ROAD
Rockfield Cotts.
MILTON ROAD
Tennis Courts
Depot
NEW BRISTOL ROAD
B3440
30
@Worle Spts. Cen.
Playing Field
Tennis Courts
Worle Community School
Play. Flds.
Mead Vale Prim. Sch.
Nightingale Ct.
LOCKING B3440 ROAD
MAYFIELD AV.
Playing Field Pav.
Baytree Ct
Hill View Ct.
LOCKING RD.
20
MEAD VALE
Worle Junct.

E
F
G
H
37
38
65
64
63
62
1
2
3
4
5
6
WICK RD.
Chapel House
Banfield Cottage
The Old House
Hodder's Farm
Mendip View
Hippisley's Farm
WICK ROAD
Banfield Farm
Ebdon Farm
Ebdon Bow Farm
Ebdon Court Farm
Ebdon
Oak Farm
Bourton
EBDON LANE
Woodspring Sch.
Manor Farm
Court Farm
Willow Fm.
LANE
Ebdon Lane Farm
BLUEBELL
CLOVER RD.
POPPY CL.
BARLEY CROSS
ACONITE CL.
WHEATFIELD
LILAC WY.
FOXGLOVE
LAVENDER CL.
TOWNSHEND
WARRILOW
STABBINS
KELSTON GDNS.
RAWLINS AV.
LOCKSBROOK RD.
PRISTON CL.
CASTLEMEAD SHOP. CEN.
Castle Batch Prim. Sch.
Lansdown Gdns.
SPINNERS END
THE FIELDERS
WANSBROUGH
KELSTON
ROSE GDS.
GAMBLETT RD.
WALFORD
TAUNTON
GRACE RD.
RICHARDS CL.
HAMBLEDON RD.
St. Georges Ct.
JESMOND RD.
Brimbleworth Farm
River Banwell
AVENUE
DUNE
FENNERS
THE SAFFRONS
HAWKSWORTH DR.
BENTLEY RD.
DEAN CL.
COULSON
GOOCH WY.
Castle Batch Recreation Ground
TUDOR ROAD
LISLE
PORTISHEAD ROAD
CANTERBURY CL.
CANTERBURY CLOSE
AUSTEN DR.
MAGDALEN WY.
BISHOP AV.
ABBOT'S CL.
WESLEY DR.
WINTER CL.
CABOT WAY
BECKET
THE LAWNS
QUEEN'S WAY
Subways
Priory Community Sch.
Playing Field
MARKET AV.
THE AVENUE
OAK CT.
REED WY.
JUBILEE WY.
OAKTREE PL.
RIVERSIDE CL.
THE BADGERS
HEDGES
St. Georges Church Prim. Sch.
BRIMBLEWORTH LA.
SAXON CT.
MEADOW PL.
NOELS SIDINGS INDUS. EST.
Wks.
Depot
ROAD
St. Georges
THE COPSE
WILLOW CLOSE
RIVER WK.
M5 MOTORWAY
M5
Comm. Cen.
TRELAWN CL.
MEADOWLANDS
THE PASTURES
COURT CL.
Old Yeo
Rhyne
BIRCH CT.
VALE CR.
STATION
MILESTONE CT.
SHEPHERD'S WY.
WILLOW
ASH
HAWTHORN
GOOSEY LA.
A370
Junction 21
RED LODGE BUS. PK.
WARLEYS LANE
LOCKING CASTLE BUS. PK.
Warehouse
BS24
SCOT ELM DR.
SCOT ELM DRIVE
TORRINGTON CRES.
STARCROSS RD.
LYNMOUTH CL.
VINE GS.
St. Clements Ct.
Prim. Sch.
Ebdon Ct.
CLOVELLY RD.
TAVISTOCK
MARLBOROUGH
APPLETREE M.
COKER RD.
NORTH WORLE SHOP. CEN.
Superstores
COMMERCIAL WY.
QUEENSWAY CENTRE
Mag. Ct.
Queensway House
BRISTOL ROAD
B3440
ROAD
DARTMOUTH CL.
OLD BRISTOL RD.
PADDOCK PARK HOMES
Bridge Farm
Ebden Lodge
SUMMER LA.
GLASTONBURY WY.
TOR CL.
PARK WAY
Worle
BLACKBERRY DR.
VERBENA WAY
LIME CL.
HOLLY CL.
ALMOND CL.
BLACKTHORN GDS.
SUMMER LANE
Diamond Court
DIAMOND BATCH
YARBURY WY.
DARMEAD
LUPIN WY.
FILERS WAY
SOMERSET AVENUE
West Wick
WILLAN PL.
BLACKBURN WY.
Weston Village
Lakeside Ct.
ROWAN PL.
Plum Tree Farm
JASMINE WY.
ELMHAM WY.
Camping Site
St. Anne's C of E Prim. Sch. (West Wick)
WEST WICK
Westacres Fm.
NEWTON WLK.
DE SALIS
The Campus
Lib.
HIGHLANDS
Superstore
Baytree Sch. & Herons Moor
WEST WICK ROUNDABOUT
CHURCHLAND WAY
21

A
B
C
D
1
2
3
4
5
6
42
43
65
64
63
62
8
24
Frost Hill
FROST HILL
FROST
TRIPPS CNR.
PARK
ROAD
BRAMLEY CL.
CADBURY FARM RD.
Cadbury Farm
Frost Hill
Hill Court
Hillside
Westover Cottage
Court Club
Rhyne
Binhay
Land Farm
Congresbury Moor
SMALLWAY
B3133
Greenholm Nurseries
Cadbury Garden Centre
Poultry Houses
Middle Elm
WESTON
A370
CONGRESBURY YEO
Withydale Farm
Moor Bridge
Stepstones Farm
OLD WESTON RD.
LANE
ROAD
STATION
ROAD
CONGRESBURY
Congresbury Bridge
BRISTOL
KENT
A370
SHEPPY'S MI.
SMALLWAY
SOUTH
GOOSEHAM MEAD
OAK FARM TOURING PARK
STATION CL.
Church Farm
GLEN YEO TER.
ST. ANDREW'S CL.
Harley Kennels
DOLEMOOR
LITTLE
CHURCH DR.
Lib.
BRIDGE FM. SQ.
Cross
BROAD ST.
HIGH B3133
Club
St. Andrew's Primary Sch.
DROVE
PAUL'S CAUSEWAY
TREE CT.
WALNUT
ORCHARD CL.
CHESTNUT
Poplar Farm
WALL
LANE
THE CAUSEWAY
STREET
Play. Flds. Pav.
Tennis Courts
STONEWELL
Brandeer Rhyne
LANE DOLEMOOR
DOLEMOOR
Playing Field
DROVE
STONEWELL GRO.
PARK RD.
DRIVE
LA.
ROAD
STONEWELL
Rookery Farm
SILVERSTONE WY.
YEW TREE PK.
YEW TREE
BS49
Weston-super-Mare
BS24
SILVER
Silver Street Farm
Meer Wall Rhyne
Crookwell Rhyne
CROOKWELL
DROVE
MOOR
Crookwell
Carditch Rhyne
Rhyne
Driving
CA

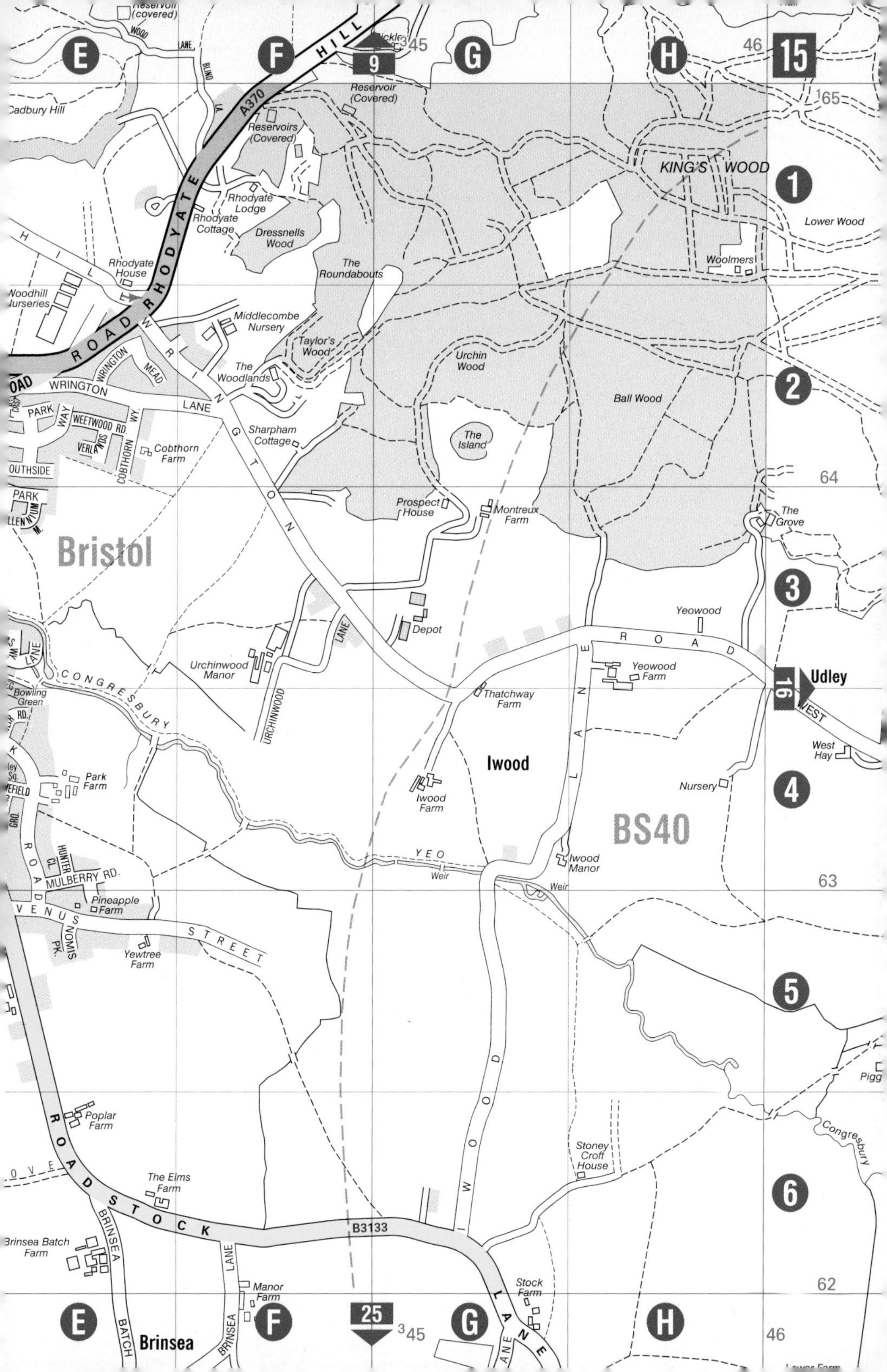
15
E
F
G
H
1
2
3
4
5
6
9
16
25
345
46
65
64
63
62
Reservoir (covered)
Reservoir (Covered)
Reservoirs (Covered)
WOOD LANE
BLIND LA.
HILL
A370
RHODYATE
ROAD
Cadbury Hill
Rhodyate Lodge
Rhodyate Cottage
Dressnells Wood
Rhodyate House
Woodhill Nurseries
The Roundabouts
Middlecombe Nursery
Taylor's Wood
The Woodlands
WRINGTON
WRINGTON LANE
WRINGTON MEAD
PARK WAY
WEETWOOD RD.
COBTHORN WY.
Cobthorn Farm
SOUTHSIDE
Sharpham Cottage
KING'S WOOD
Lower Wood
Woolmers
Urchin Wood
Ball Wood
The Island
Prospect House
Montreux Farm
The Grove
Bristol
Depot
LANE
URCHINWOOD
Urchinwood Manor
CONGRESBURY
Bowling Green
Yeowood
ROAD
Yeowood Farm
Thatchway Farm
Udley
WEST
West Hay
Iwood
Iwood Farm
Nursery
BS40
Park Farm
HUNTER CL.
MULBERRY RD.
YEO
Weir
Iwood Manor
Pineapple Farm
VENUS STREET
Yewtree Farm
Pigg
Congresbury
Poplar Farm
The Elms Farm
Stoney Croft House
STOCK
B3133
WOOD LANE
Brinsea Batch Farm
BRINSEA BATCH
LANE
Manor Farm
Stock Farm
Brinsea
BRINSEA
Lower Farm

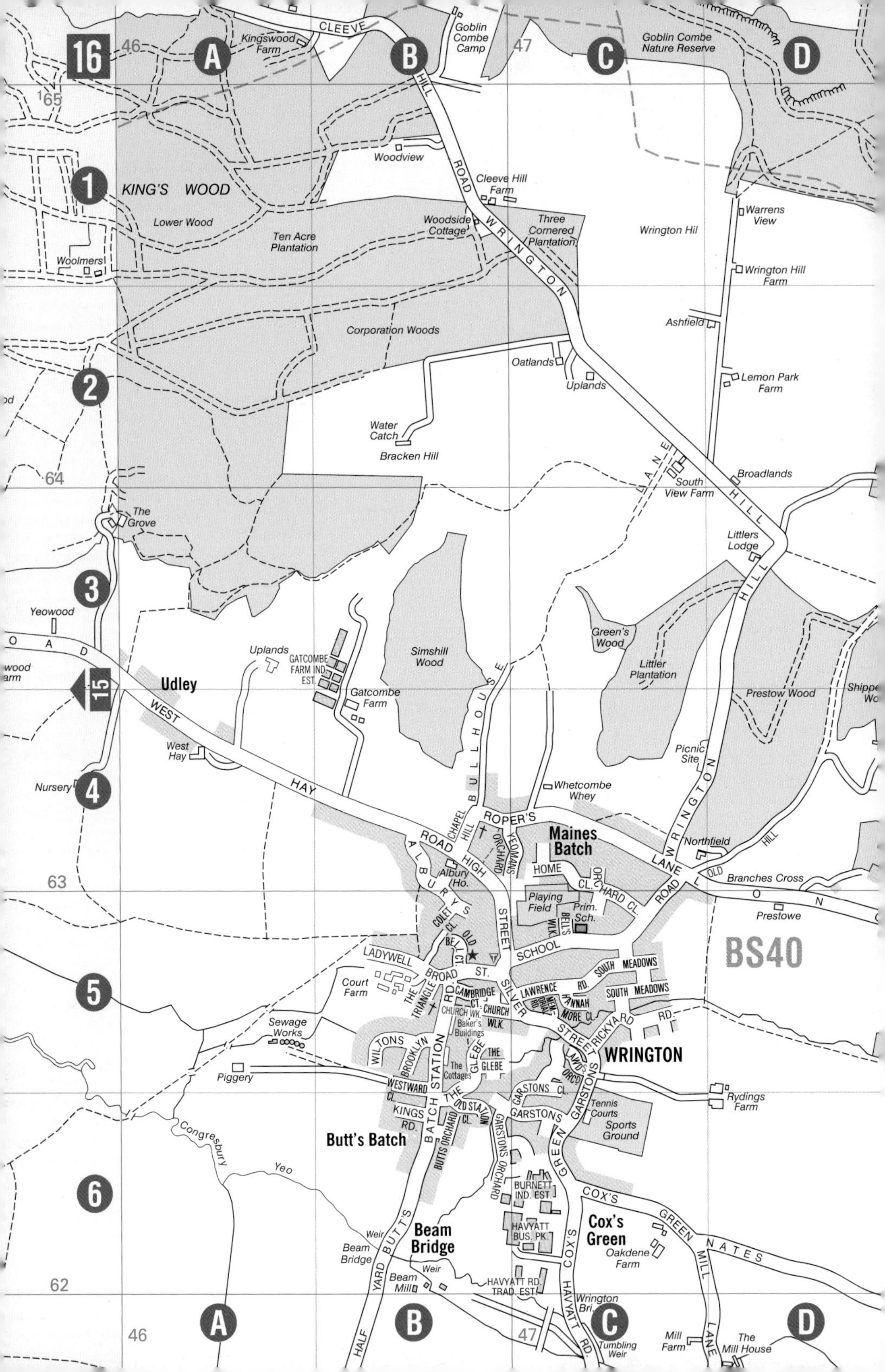

16
46
47
165
64
63
62
A
B
C
D
1
2
3
4
5
6
15
CLEEVE
Kingswood Farm
Goblin Combe Camp
Goblin Combe Nature Reserve
KING'S WOOD
Lower Wood
Ten Acre Plantation
Woolmers
Woodview
Cleeve Hill Farm
Woodside Cottage
Three Cornered Plantation
WRINGTON
ROAD
HILL
Wrington Hil
Warrens View
Wrington Hill Farm
Ashfield
Corporation Woods
Oatlands
Uplands
Lemon Park Farm
Water Catch
Bracken Hill
Broadlands
LANE
South View Farm
The Grove
Littlers Lodge
Yeowood
Green's Wood
Littler Plantation
Simshill Wood
Uplands
GATCOMBE FARM IND. EST.
Gatcombe Farm
Udley
WEST
HAY
West Hay
Nursery
Prestow Wood
Picnic Site
BULLHOUSE
Whetcombe Whey
CHAPEL HILL
ROPER'S
YEOMANS
ORCHARD
Maines Batch
HOME
ORCHARD CL.
Northfield
Branches Cross
OLD
Prestowe
ALBURYS
Albury Ho.
HIGH STREET
Playing Field
Prim. Sch.
BELL'S WLK.
SCHOOL
COLET CL.
BELL CT.
OLD
BS40
LADYWELL
BROAD ST.
SILVER
SOUTH MEADOWS
Court Farm
THE TRIANGLE
CAMBRIDGE CT.
LAWRENCE RD.
HANNAH MORE CL.
RICKYARD RD.
CHURCH WK.
CHURCH WLK.
Baker's Buildings
Sewage Works
WILTONS
BROOKLYN
STATION
THE GLEBE
STREET
WRINGTON
Piggery
The Cottages
WESTWARD CL.
KINGS RD.
BATCH
THE OLD STATION CL.
GARSTONS CL.
GARSTONS
Tennis Courts
Sports Ground
Rydings Farm
Butt's Batch
BUTTS ORCHARD
GARSTONS ORCHARD
GREEN
Congresbury
Yeo
BURNETT IND. EST.
COX'S
Cox's Green
NATES
HAVYATT BUS. PK.
Oakdene Farm
Weir
Beam Bridge
BUTT'S
Beam Bridge
Beam Mill
HAVYATT RD. TRAD. EST.
Wrington Bri.
YARD
HALF
HAVYATT RD.
Mill Farm
The Mill House
Tumbling Weir
LANE
MILL

E
F
G
H
Abspit Pond
North Hill
49
350
165
WINTERS LANE
BS48
GOBLIN COMBE
Highfield
Goblin Coombe Farm
Spying Copse
Broadfield Farm
Springfields
1
2
High Wood
64
Reservoir (Covered)
Bristol
Hailstones Farm
3
Meeting House Farm
Cottage Farm
To Bristol International Airport 1.5 miles
Hortswood Farm
Hortswood Cottage
Raglan Farm
HILL
Little Horts Wood
Burnt House Farm
Vosper Lodge
REDCROFT
4
REDACRE
CHURCH ROAD
CHURCH CT.
A38
Tucker's Grove
Horts Wood
THE POUND
Redhill
LANE
Chancellor's Farm
63
East Lodge
Whitley Coppice
Rockdunder
Rockdunder Lodge
LYE
Scars Farm
Stable Cottage
Bottenham Coppice
Chancellor's Cottage
5
HOLE
Boxbush Cotel
PUMP LANE
Lye Hole
LANE
SUTTON LA.
Lye Cross
RED
Reservoir (Covered)
Lye Hole Piggery
UNDER
Boxbush Farm
ROAD
PIGEON
LA.
LYE CROSS
6
Lye Cross Farm
Pigeon House Farm
CRIBB'S
Cribb's Farm
62
BROOK LODGE TOURING CARAVAN & CAMPING PARK
COWSLIP GRN
Brook Cottages
Cowslip Green
E
F
49
G
H
350

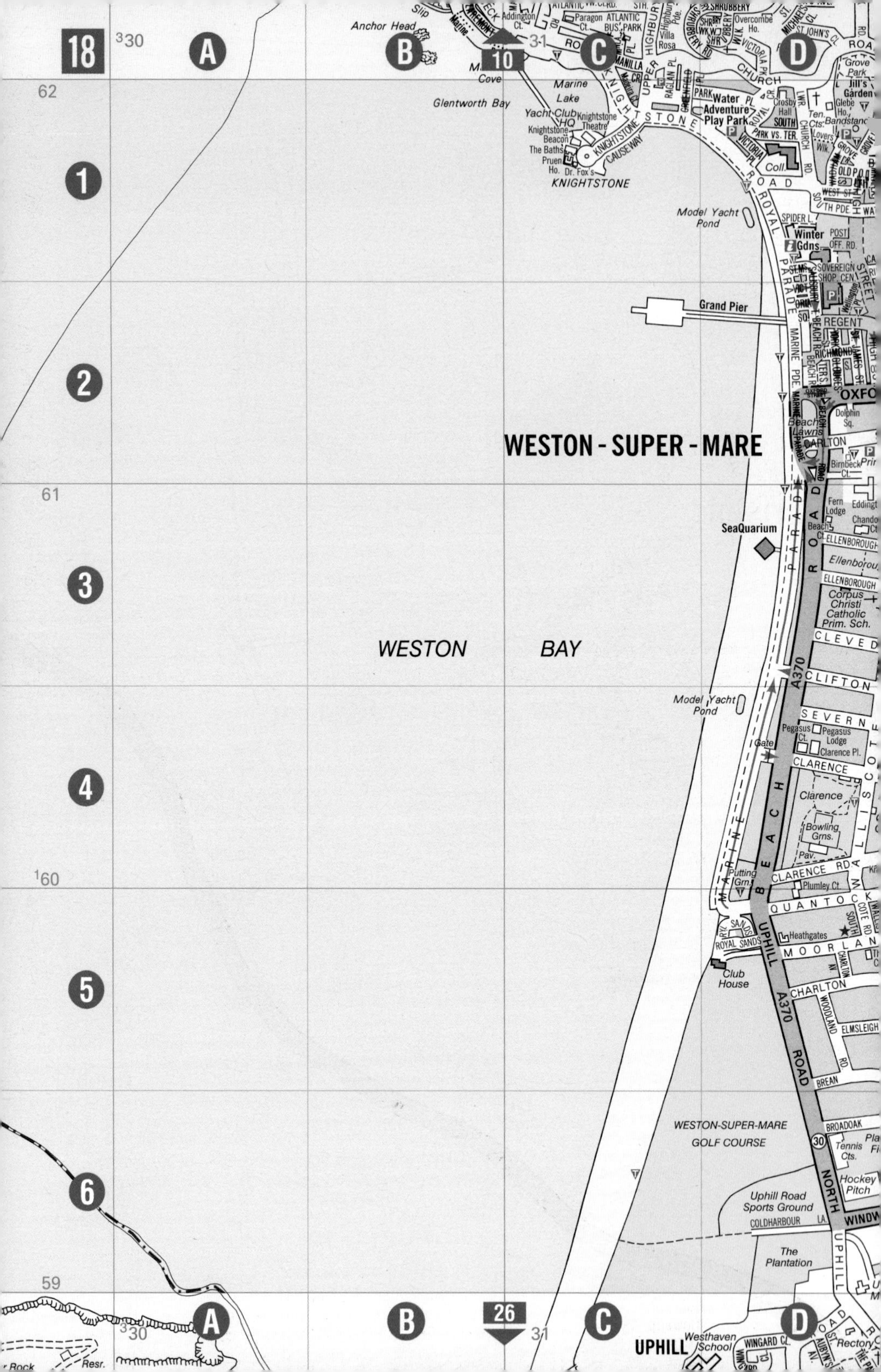
WESTON - SUPER - MARE
WESTON BAY
Anchor Head
Glentworth Bay
Marine Lake
Yacht Club HQ
Knightstone Theatre
Knightstone Beacon
The Baths
Pruen Ho.
Dr. Fox's
KNIGHTSTONE
KNIGHTSTONE CAUSEWAY
Water Adventure Play Park
Model Yacht Pond
Winter Gdns
Grand Pier
ROYAL PARADE
MARINE PDE.
Beach Lawns
SeaQuarium
Corpus Christi Catholic Prim. Sch.
Clarence Bowling Grns.
Putting Grn.
Club House
ROYAL SANDS
Heathgates
WESTON-SUPER-MARE GOLF COURSE
Uphill Road Sports Ground
COLDHARBOUR LA.
The Plantation
UPHILL
Westhaven School
WINGARD CL.
Rectory
BEACH ROAD
UPHILL ROAD NORTH
A370
CLARENCE RD.
CHARLTON
MOORLAND
QUANTOCK
SEVERN
CLIFTON
ELLENBOROUGH
BREAN
BROADOAK
ELMSLEIGH
WOODLAND RD.
Tennis Cts.
Hockey Pitch
Plumley Ct.
Pegasus Ct.
Pegasus Lodge
Clarence Pl.
Fern Lodge
Beach Ct.
Birnbeck Ct.
Dolphin Sq.
REGENT
RICHMOND
CARLTON
SOVEREIGN SHOP. CEN.
POST OFF. RD.
Crosby Hall
Coll.
Jill's Garden
Bandstand
Lovers Wlk.
Grove Park
WEST ST.
SOUTH PDE.
SPIDER L.
Paragon Ct.
ATLANTIC BUS. PARK
Addington Ct.
Overcombe Ho.
Villa Rosa
MANILLA CR.
UPPER HIGHBURY
RAGLAN PL.
CHURCH
Gate
Resr.
Rock
A
B
C
D
1
2
3
4
5
6
62
61
^{1}60
59
^{3}30
31
10
26

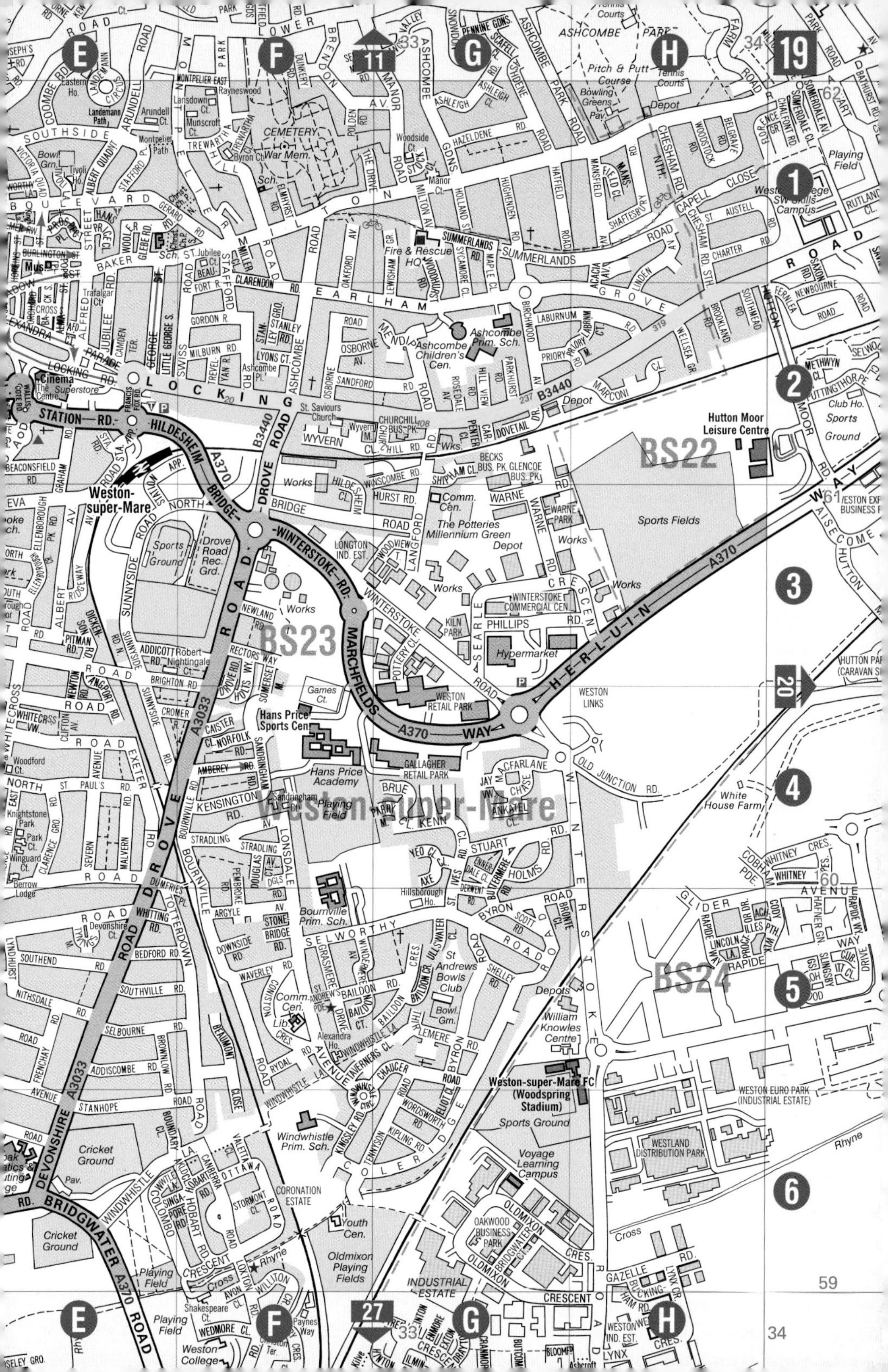
19
11
20
27
E
F
G
H
1
2
3
4
5
6
33
34
59
60
61
62
BS22
BS23
BS24
Weston-super-Mare
Ashcombe Park
Pitch & Putt Course
Tennis Courts
Bowling Greens
Pav.
Depot
Cemetery
War Mem.
Sch.
Fire & Rescue HQ
Ashcombe Prim. Sch.
Ashcombe Children's Cen.
Weston College SW Skills Campus
Playing Field
Hutton Moor Leisure Centre
Club Ho.
Sports Ground
Sports Fields
Mus.
Cinema
The Centre
Superstore
Weston-super-Mare
St. Saviours Church
Wyvern M.
Churchill Bus. Pk.
Becks Bus. Pk.
Glencoe Bus. Pk.
Works
Comm. Cen.
The Potteries Millennium Green
Depot
Longton Ind. Est.
Kiln Park
Winterstoke Commercial Cen.
Hypermarket
Drove Road Rec. Grd.
Games Ct.
Hans Price Sports Cen.
Hans Price Academy
Weston Retail Park
Gallagher Retail Park
Weston Links
White House Farm
Hutton Park (Caravan Site)
Weston Exp Business Park
Playing Field
Bournville Prim. Sch.
Hillsborough Ho.
St Andrews Bowls Club
Bowl. Grn.
Comm. Cen.
Lib.
Alexandra Ho.
Depots
William Knowles Centre
Weston-super-Mare FC (Woodspring Stadium)
Sports Ground
Voyage Learning Campus
Windwhistle Prim. Sch.
Coronation Estate
Youth Cen.
Oldmixon Playing Fields
Oakwood Business Park
Industrial Estate
Weston Euro Park (Industrial Estate)
Westland Distribution Park
Rhyne
Cross Rhyne
Weston Ind. Est.
Cricket Ground
Pav.
Playing Field
Weston College
Paynes Way
Knightstone Park
Winguard Ct.
Berrow Lodge
Woodford Ct.
Devonshire Ct.
Locking Rd.
Station Rd.
Hildesheim Bridge
A370
B3440
A3033
Drove Road
Winterstoke Rd.
Marchfields
A370 Way
Herluin Way
Winterstoke Road
Summerlands Rd.
Earlham Grove
Milton Road
Ashcombe Road
Southside
Boulevard
Baker St.
Alexandra Parade
Bridge Road
Sunnyside Road
Brighton Rd.
Kensington Rd.
Selworthy Road
Byron Road
Coleridge Road
Windwhistle Road
Devonshire Road
Bridgwater Road
Oldmixon Cres.
Old Junction Rd.
Glider Avenue
Moor Lane
Hutton Moor Road
Marconi Cl.
Dovetail Dr.
Wyvern Cl.
Bourneville Rd.
Totterdown Rd.

A
B
C
D
1
2
3
4
5
6
12
19
28
34
335
62
61
160
59
BS22
BS23
BS24
Weston-super-Mare
LOCKING
HUTTON
Weston Milton Station
Weston College SW Skills Campus
Playing Field
Hutton Moor Leisure Centre
Club Ho.
Sports Ground
WESTON EXPRESS BUSINESS PARK
Refuse Transfer Station
Factory
Reservoir
HUTTON PARK (CARAVAN SITE)
SITE OF WESTON AIRFIELD (Disused)
The Helicopter Museum
WESTON BUSINESS PARK
OAKTREE PARK (CARAVAN SITE)
West End Farm
Drove Farm
Lodwell Farm
Tennis Courts
Nursery
Plumley Park
Locking Bridge
Sports Field
Play. Fld.
WESTON EURO PARK (INDUSTRIAL ESTATE)
Rhyne
Cross
Hutton and Locking Rhyne
FLOWERDOWN BRIDGE
A370
A371
B3440
B3368
HERLUIN WAY
LOCKING ROAD
LOCKING MOOR RD.
SOMERSET
MOOR LANE
LANEYS DROVE
BEAUFIGHTER RD.
AVENUE
WAY
ELM
MOORCROFT
VERELAND
HOLMFIELD RD.

West Wick
Camping Site
St. Anne's C of E Prim. Sch. (West Wick)
Westacres Fm.
Weston Village
The Campus
Liby
Baytree Sch. & Herons Moor Academy
Superstore
WEST WICK ROUNDABOUT
CHURCHLAND WY.
A370
Ivy Cottage
SUMMER LANE
WOLVERSHILL
M5 MOTORWAY
M5
Old Yeo Rhyne
Refinery
Gobbles Farm
ETON LANE
Ivy House Farm
Golf Driving Range
Banwell
Wolvershill Manor
WOLVERSHILL INDUSTRIAL ESTATE
BS29
Locking Head Cottages
Nursery
LOCKING HEAD DROVE
Locking Head Farm
Grumblepill
Locking Parklands
Batch Farm
Chestnut Farm
Playground
ANSON ROAD
OXFORD SQUARE
RUSSELL
LEEDHAM ROAD
Tennis Courts
LOWER PARADE GROUND ROAD
Rhyne
SUMMER LA.
Myrtle Farm
Laurel Farm
LOCKING FARM INDUSTRIAL ESTATE
HOMEFIELD IND. EST.
A371 ROAD
Stadium (Disused)
POST OFFICE ROAD
BOWEN RD.
FARNBOROUGH
CRANWELL RD.
CHESHIRE
HANNAH DR.
PARKES RD.
Locking Primary School
Hall
Plumley Cr.
THE GREEN
LYCHGATE PK.
MENDIP RI.
BIRCH CL.
BANWELL B3368 ROAD
Connemara
OLD
Church Farm
BURY
MENDIP
FLOWERDOWN
TOWER HILL
PINETREE RD.
TRENCHARD
PORTAL RD.
Tall Timbers
Cave View
Club
Devils Elbow Farm
Perries
KNIGHTCOTT INDUSTRIAL ESTATE
Longcroft
Karibu
THE BANWELL ROAD
Wingfield House
Nursery Gardens
Elborough
Elborough Farm
CEDERN AVENUE
SHADOW WK.
BLUE WATER DR.
LLOYD CL.
Elborough Wood
Hill View Farm
Hillend Farm
Hillend
Manor Farm
The Caves
E
F
G
H
1
2
3
4
5
6
13
22
29
37
38
59
60
61
62

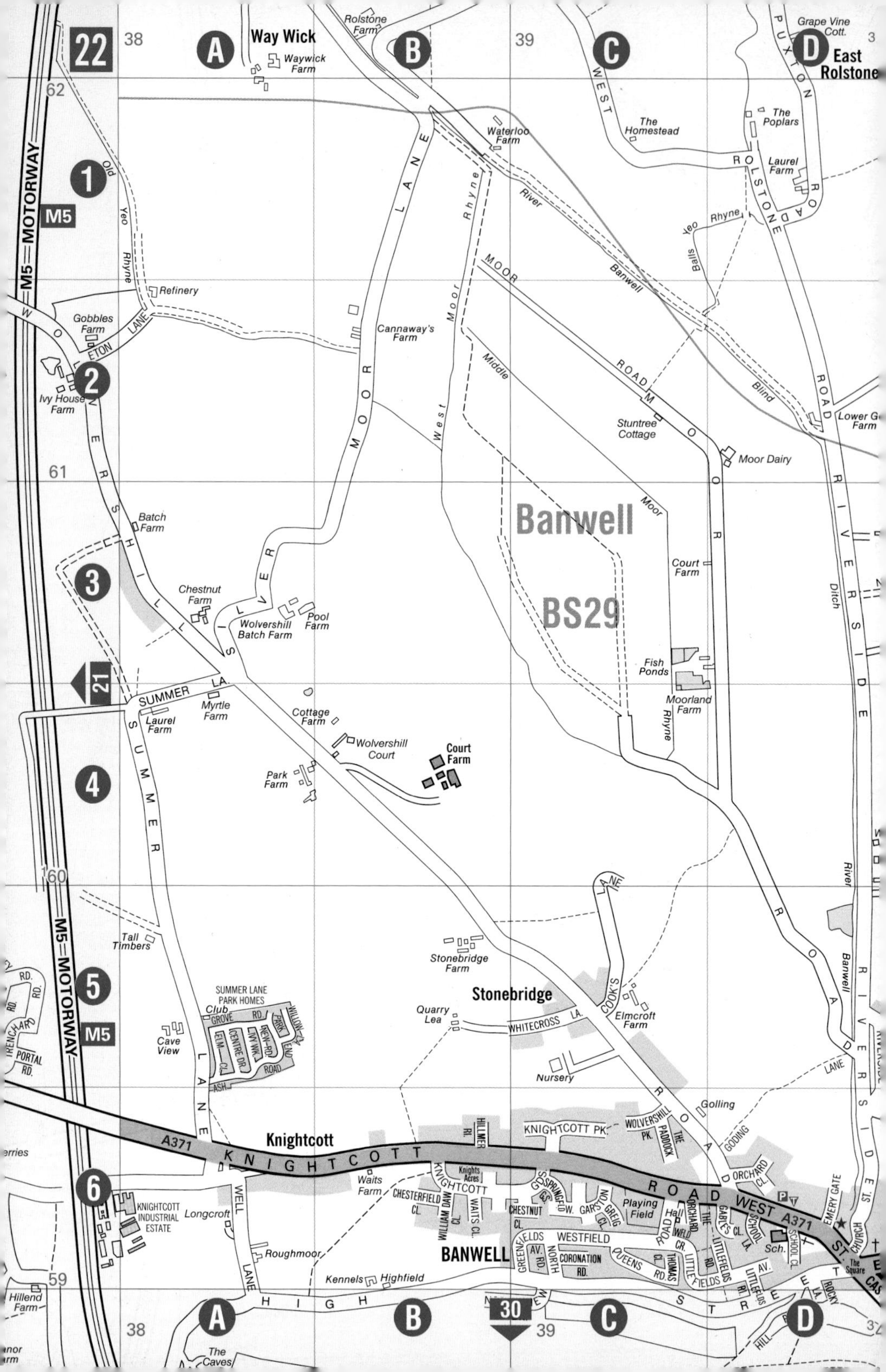
38
39
A
B
C
D
Way Wick
Waywick Farm
Rolstone Farm
Grape Vine Cott.
East Rolstone
PUXTON ROAD
WEST
The Homestead
The Poplars
ROLSTONE
Laurel Farm
Waterloo Farm
62
61
160
59
1
2
3
4
5
6
M5 MOTORWAY
M5
Old Yeo Rhyne
Refinery
Gobbles Farm
WOOLVERSHILL
ETON LANE
Ivy House Farm
MOOR LANE
Cannaway's Farm
West Moor Rhyne
River Banwell
Yeo Rhyne
Balls
MOOR ROAD
Middle
Blind
Stuntree Cottage
Moor Dairy
Lower G Farm
RIVERSIDE
Ditch
West
Moor
Banwell
BS29
Court Farm
Fish Ponds
Moorland Farm
Rhyne
Batch Farm
SILVER
Chestnut Farm
Wolvershill Batch Farm
Pool Farm
21
SUMMER LA.
Myrtle Farm
Laurel Farm
Cottage Farm
Wolvershill Court
Court Farm
Park Farm
SUMMER LANE
LANE
COOK'S
River
Banwell
Tall Timbers
Stonebridge Farm
Stonebridge
Quarry Lea
WHITECROSS LA.
Elmcroft Farm
Nursery
SUMMER LANE PARK HOMES
Club
GROVE RD.
ELM CL.
CENTRE DR.
IVY WK.
NEW RD.
PARK END
WILLOW
ROAD
ASH
Cave View
RD.
RD.
RD.
TRENCHARD
PORTAL RD.
Golling
GODING
LANE
WOLVERSHILL ROAD
A371 KNIGHTCOTT ROAD WEST A371
Knightcott
HILLMER RI.
KNIGHTCOTT PK.
WOLVERSHILL PK.
THE PADDOCK
ORCHARD CL.
EMERY GATE
CHURCH ST.
WELL LANE
Knights Acres
Waits Farm
KNIGHTCOTT
CHESTERFIELD CL.
WILLIAM DAW CL.
WAITS CL.
CHESTNUT CL.
SPRINGFIELD
W. GARSTON
NO GREIG
Playing Field
Hall
ORCHARD
THE LITTLEFIELDS
GABLES CL.
SCHOOL LA.
SCHOOL CL.
Sch.
The Square
KNIGHTCOTT INDUSTRIAL ESTATE
Longcroft
Roughmoor
BANWELL
GREENFIELDS
AV. RD.
NORTH
WESTFIELD
CORONATION RD.
QUEENS RD.
THOMAS CL.
WESTFIELD CR.
LITTLE FIELDS
LITTLEFIELDS AV.
ROCKY
HIGH STREET
Kennels
Highfield
HILL
Hillend Farm
The Caves
30
37
3

Boxbush Farm
BOX BUSH LANE
Boxbush Stables
Depot
PUXTON LANE
HAVAGE DROVE
MEER WALL
Nut Tree Farm
Nye
Rhyne
DROVE
Nye Farm
Rookery Farm East
Rockers
Weston-super-Mare
BS24
Towerhead
Sandmead
WAY NYE
Droveway Bridge
Bridge Farm
Droveway Farm
MEAD LANE
Mead Farm
Westleigh Farm
Brook
Depot
STATION ROAD
A368
ROMAN RD
APIL
PEGASUS PL
The Russets
Sherwood
Towerhead Farm
Towerhead
Depot
Darlisette House
SANDFORD
ORCHARD DR
BRMLY CL
YEW TREE GDS
SOMERVILLE
WINNOWING END
SANDMEAD
Winscombe
BS25
Depot
EASTERMEAD LANE
Eastermead Farm
A368 ST. TOWERHEAD ROAD
Banwell Plain
Banwell Wood
Depot
Sandford Batch
HILL
STH. CROFT
SOUTH HILL
QUARRY RD
41
42
62
61
60
59

24

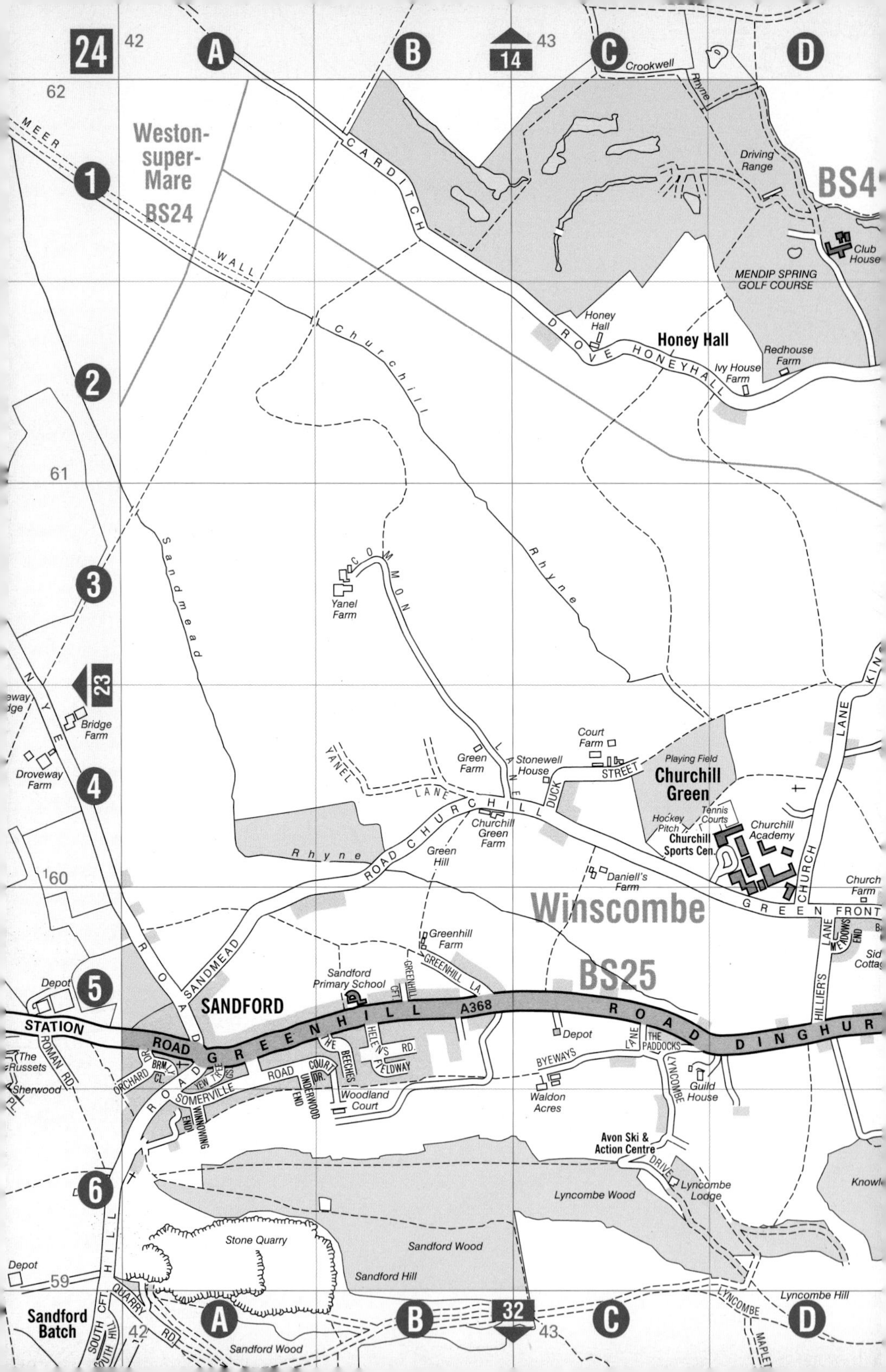

42
43
A
B
C
D
14
23
32
62
61
60
59
1
2
3
4
5
6
Weston-super-Mare
BS24
MEER WALL
CARDITCH DROVE
Crookwell Rhyne
Driving Range
BS4
Club House
MENDIP SPRING GOLF COURSE
Honey Hall
Honey Hall
HONEYHALL
Redhouse Farm
Ivy House Farm
Churchill Rhyne
Sandmead
COMMON LANE
Yanel Farm
NYE ROAD
Bridge Farm
Droveway Farm
YANEL LANE
Green Farm
Stonewell House
Court Farm
DUCK STREET
Playing Field
Churchill Green
Tennis Courts
Hockey Pitch
Churchill Academy
Churchill Sports Cen.
CHURCHILL ROAD
Churchill Green Farm
Green Hill
Rhyne
Daniell's Farm
Winscombe
CHURCH LANE
Church Farm
GREEN FRONT
MEADOWS END
HILLIER'S LANE
Greenhill Farm
GREENHILL LA.
BS25
SANDMEAD
Sandford Primary School
SANDFORD
Depot
STATION ROAD
GREENHILL ROAD
A368
DINGHURST ROAD
ROMAN RD.
The Russets
Sherwood
ORCHARD DR.
BRMLY CL.
YEW TREES
SOMERVILLE ROAD
WINNOWING END
UNDERWOOD END
COURT DR.
THE BEECHES
HELENS RD.
FELDWAY
Woodland Court
Depot
BYEWAYS
Waldon Acres
LANE
THE PADDOCKS
LYNCOMBE
Guild House
Avon Ski & Action Centre
DRIVE
Lyncombe Lodge
Lyncombe Wood
Knowle
Stone Quarry
Sandford Wood
Sandford Hill
HILL ROAD
Depot
QUARRY RD.
SOUTH CFT.
SOUTH HILL
Sandford Batch
Sandford Wood
LYNCOMBE
Lyncombe Hill
MAPLE

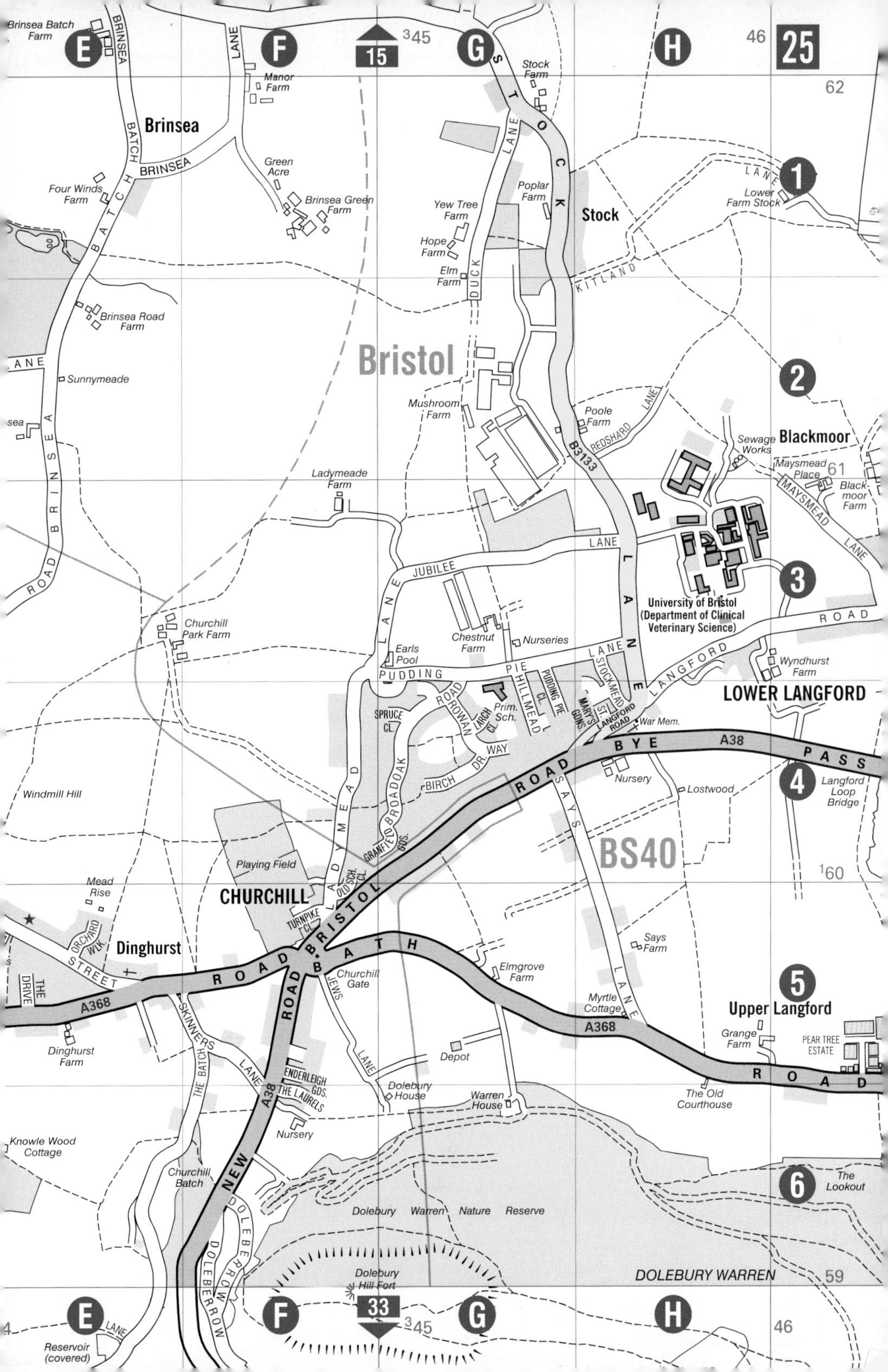
15
33
E
F
G
H
1
2
3
4
5
6
345
46
62
61
60
59
Brinsea Batch Farm
Manor Farm
Stock Farm
Brinsea
Green Acre
Brinsea Green Farm
Four Winds Farm
Poplar Farm
Yew Tree Farm
Hope Farm
Elm Farm
Stock
Lower Farm Stock
Brinsea Road Farm
Sunnymeade
Bristol
Mushroom Farm
Poole Farm
Sewage Works
Blackmoor
Maysmead Place
Blackmoor Farm
Ladymeade Farm
University of Bristol (Department of Clinical Veterinary Science)
Churchill Park Farm
Chestnut Farm
Nurseries
Earls Pool
Wyndhurst Farm
LOWER LANGFORD
Prim. Sch.
War Mem.
Nursery
Lostwood
Langford Loop Bridge
Windmill Hill
BS40
Playing Field
Mead Rise
CHURCHILL
Dinghurst
Churchill Gate
Says Farm
Elmgrove Farm
Myrtle Cottage
Upper Langford
Grange Farm
PEAR TREE ESTATE
Dinghurst Farm
Depot
Dolebury House
Warren House
The Old Courthouse
ENDERLEIGH GDS.
THE LAURELS
Nursery
Knowle Wood Cottage
Churchill Batch
The Lookout
Dolebury Warren Nature Reserve
Dolebury Hill Fort
DOLEBURY WARREN
Reservoir (covered)
BRINSEA BATCH
BRINSEA
BRINSEA ROAD
LANE
STOCK LANE
DUCK LANE
KITLAND
B3133
REDSHARD LANE
MAYSMEAD LANE
JUBILEE LANE
LANGFORD ROAD
PUDDING PIE LANE
HILLMEAD
PUDDING PIE CL.
ST. MARY'S GDNS.
STOCKMEAD
LANGFORD ROAD
SPRUCE CL.
ROWAN ROAD
LARCH CL.
BIRCH DR.
WAY
BROADOAK
GRANFIELD GDS.
LADYMEAD
OLD SCH. CL.
BRISTOL ROAD
ROAD BYE PASS
A38
SAYS LANE
TURNPIKE CL.
ORCHARD WLK.
STREET
THE DRIVE
A368
BATH ROAD
JEWS LANE
SKINNERS LANE
THE BATCH
NEW ROAD
DOLEBERROW

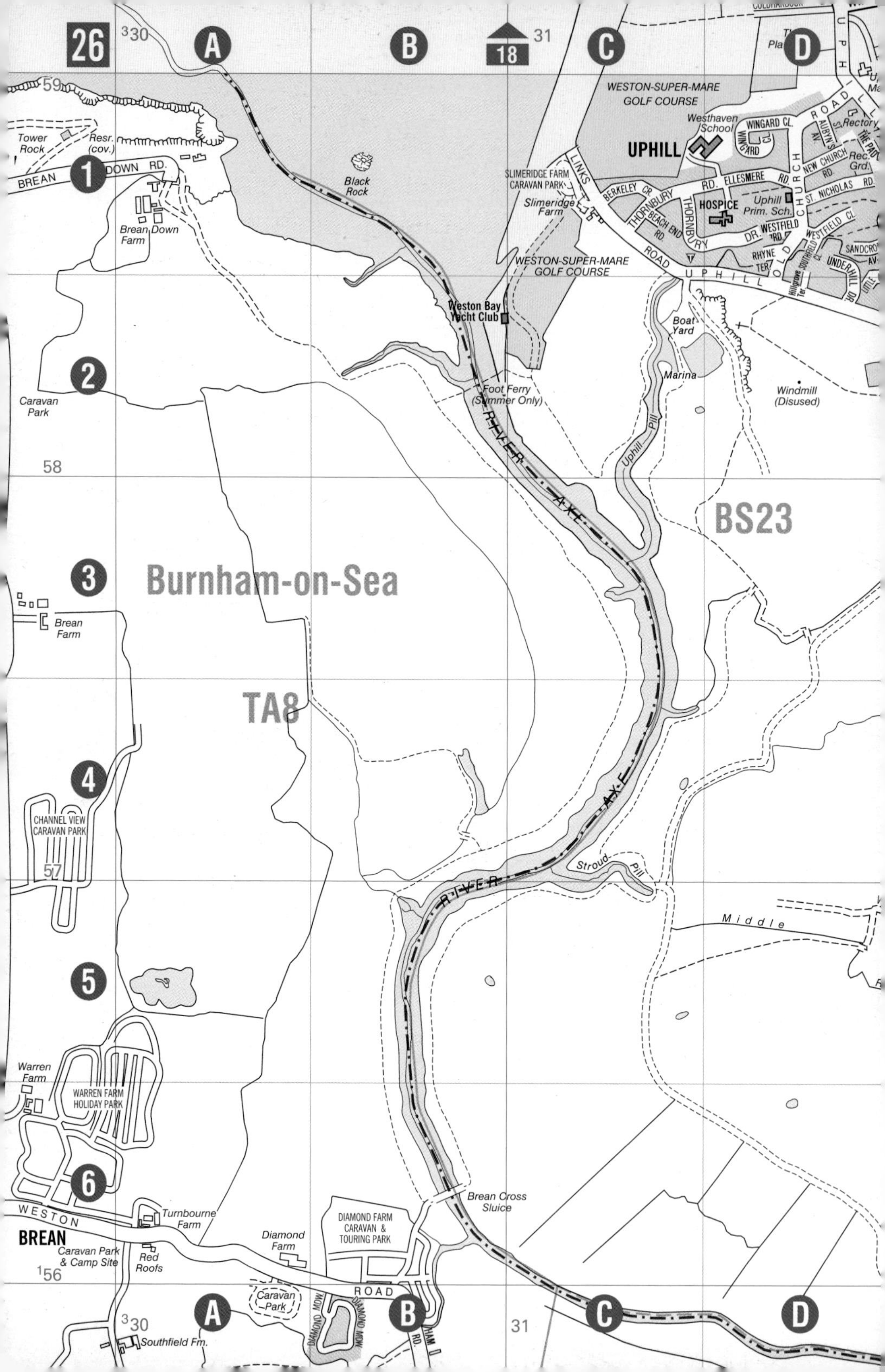

A
B
18
31
C
D
330
59
58
57
156
Tower Rock
Resr. (cov.)
BREAN DOWN RD.
Brean Down Farm
Black Rock
WESTON-SUPER-MARE GOLF COURSE
Westhaven School
UPHILL
WINGARD CL.
Rectory
SLIMERIDGE FARM CARAVAN PARK
Slimeridge Farm
LINKS
BERKELEY CR.
THORNBURY RD.
ELLESMERE RD.
HOSPICE
Uphill Prim. Sch.
NEW CHURCH RD.
ST. NICHOLAS RD.
BEACH END RD.
WESTFIELD DR.
WESTFIELD CL.
RHYNE TER.
OLD CHURCH ROAD
UPHILL ROAD
UNDERHILL DR.
Hillgrove Ter.
Rec. Grd.
Weston Bay Yacht Club
Boat Yard
Marina
Windmill (Disused)
Foot Ferry (Summer Only)
RIVER AXE
Uphill Pill
BS23
Caravan Park
Burnham-on-Sea
Brean Farm
TA8
CHANNEL VIEW CARAVAN PARK
Stroud Pill
Middle
Warren Farm
WARREN FARM HOLIDAY PARK
Brean Cross Sluice
WESTON
BREAN
Turnbourne Farm
Caravan Park & Camp Site
Red Roofs
Diamond Farm
DIAMOND FARM CARAVAN & TOURING PARK
ROAD
Caravan Park
DIAMOND MDW.
Southfield Fm.

Weston-super-Mare
BS24
Oldmixon
BLEADON
Purn
WESTON GENERAL HOSPITAL
UCC
North Somerset Acad. (Med. Sch.)
Weston College (University Campus)
Playing Field
Cricket Ground
INDUSTRIAL ESTATE
OAKWOOD BUSINESS PARK
WESTON IND. EST.
Youth Cen.
Oldmixon Play Field
Oldmixon Prim. Sch.
Broadway Lodge
Oldmixon Bridge
The Tips
MANOR FARM CARAVAN PARK
Manor Farm
UPHILL PARK HOMES
Uphill Grange
Devil's Bri.
Hay Wood
Oldmixon Copse
Totterdown Farm
Manor House
Reservoir (Covered)
Highcroft
HILLCOTE
White Barns
Nursery
Coombe Farm
Purn Hill
Purn House Farm
Purn Farm
PURN HOLIDAY PARK
Mendip Model Motor Racing Circuit
Summerways Bridge
BLEADON LEVEL
Works
Bleadon Bridge
NORTH SOMERSET
SEDGEMOOR
RIVER AXE
North Rhyne
Great Rhyne
BRIDGWATER ROAD
A370
BROADWAY
OLDMIXON ROAD
GRANGE ROAD
SOUTH BLEADON
BURNHAM DRIVE
TOTTERDOWN
ROMAN HILL
CELTIC WAY
ROAD
PURN LANE
BLEADON ROAD
ACCOMMODATION ROAD
WAYACRE DROVE
EAST MEAD DROVE
BRIDGE RD.
BLEADON MILL
THE CRESCENT
CORONATION RD.
WINTERSTOKE ROAD
AVENUE
BROMPTON RD.
MANOR GRANGE
CHESTNUT WAY
E F G H
1 2 3 4 5 6
33 34
56 57 58 59
19
28

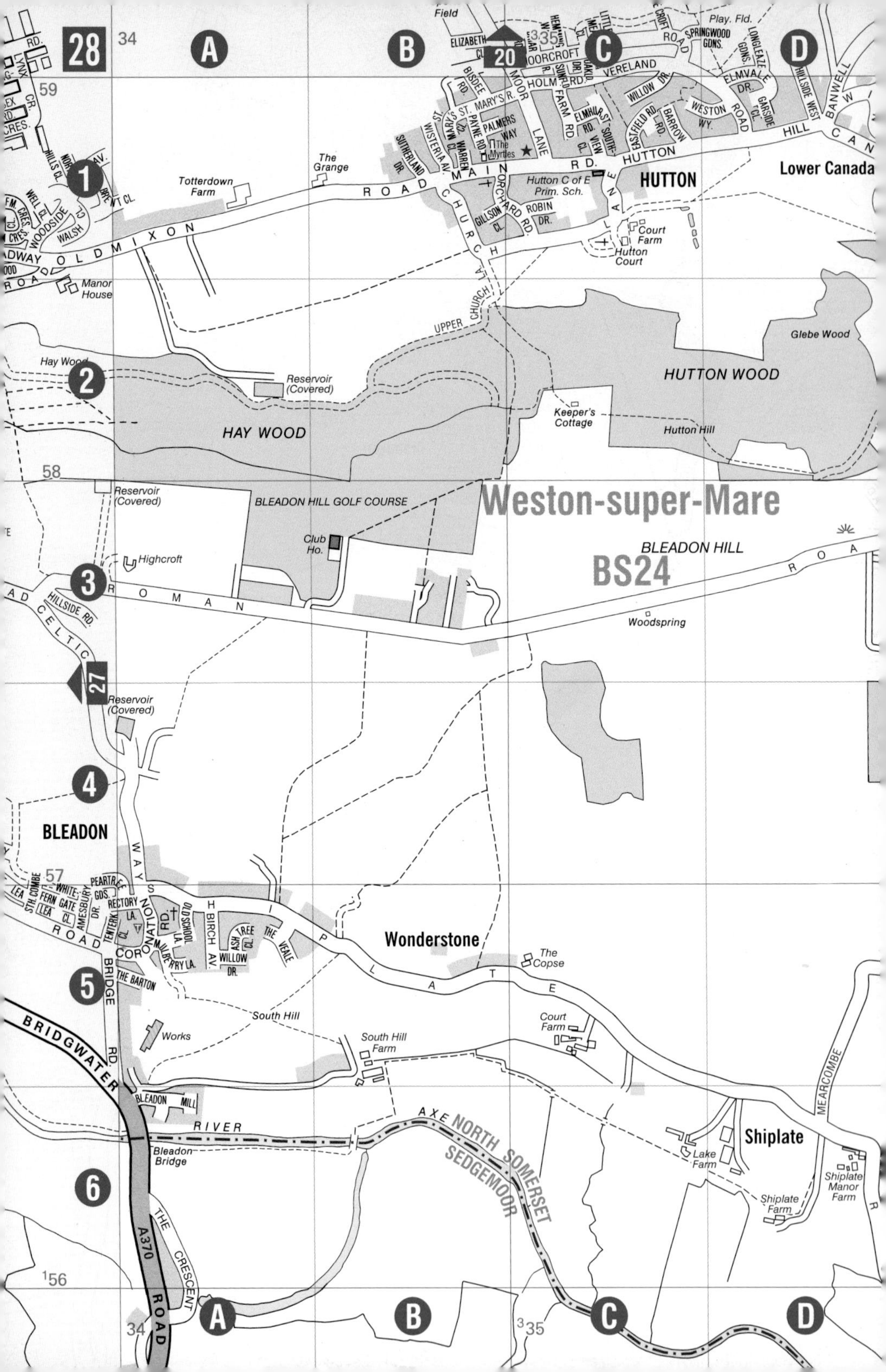

A
B
C
D
1
2
3
4
5
6
34
335
59
58
57
156
20
27
Weston-super-Mare
BS24
HUTTON
Lower Canada
BLEADON
Wonderstone
Shiplate
HUTTON WOOD
HAY WOOD
Glebe Wood
Hutton Hill
Hay Wood
BLEADON HILL
BLEADON HILL GOLF COURSE
Club Ho.
Reservoir (Covered)
Totterdown Farm
The Grange
Manor House
Hutton C of E Prim. Sch.
Court Farm
Hutton Court
Keeper's Cottage
Highcroft
Woodspring
The Myrtles
The Copse
South Hill
South Hill Farm
Works
Bleadon Bridge
BLEADON MILL
Lake Farm
Shiplate Farm
Shiplate Manor Farm
Play. Fld.
Field
OLDMIXON ROAD
MAIN ROAD
HUTTON RD.
HUTTON HILL
ROMAN ROAD
CELTIC WAY
HILLSIDE RD.
UPPER CHURCH LA.
CHURCH LANE
MOOR LANE
VERELAND
MOORCROFT
HOLM RD.
ELMVALE DR.
HILLSIDE WEST
BANWELL
WESTON ROAD
WESTON WY.
BARROW RD.
EASTFIELD RD.
WILLOW DR.
SPRINGWOOD GDNS.
LONGLEAZE GDNS.
GARSIDE CL.
ELIZABETH CL.
ORCHARD RD.
GILLSON CL.
ROBIN DR.
PALMERS WAY
PAYNE RD.
WARREN CL.
ST. MARY'S R.
WISTERIA AV.
SUTHERLAND DR.
BISDEE RD.
WOODSIDE
WALSH CL.
BRENT CL.
WELL CL.
LYNX CR.
HILLS CL.
BRIDGWATER ROAD
A370
THE CRESCENT
BRIDGE RD.
THE BARTON
CORONATION RD.
MULBERRY LA.
RECTORY LA.
BIRCH AV.
ASH TREE CL.
THE VEALE
WILLOW DR.
SCHOOL LA.
AMESBURY DR.
PEARTREE GDS.
FERN GATE
LEA CL.
STH. COMBE
PLATE
SHIPLATE
MEARCOMBE
RIVER AXE
NORTH SOMERSET
SEDGEMOOR

29
21
30
Elborough
Elborough Farm
Wingfield House
Nursery Gardens
Elborough Wood
Hill View Farm
Hillend
Hillend Farm
Manor Farm
INDUSTRIAL ESTATE
M5 MOTORWAY
M5
The Caves
Benthills Wood
Windmill Farm
Elborough Hill
The Coombe
Upper Canada
East Hill
Elborough Wood
BRIDEWELL LANE
BRIDEWELL LA.
Canada Farm
Christon Hill
COOMBE HILL
Christon Plantation
Little Common
Barleycombe
Leaze Cottage
Keeper's Cottage
CHRISTON HILL
Reservoir (Covered)
Shiplett Hill Farm
Manor Farm
FLAGSTAFF RD.
BANWELL ROAD
WESTON LA.
Hillfield Farm
Christon
Hamwood
Galtons
Loxton Hill
SHIPLATE SLAIT
Axbridge
Oakes Farm
BS26
CHRISTON ROAD
Loxton Wood
Shiplate Wood
Church Farm
Loxton
BARTON RD.
E
F
G
H
1
2
3
4
5
6
37
38
56
57
58
59

INDUSTRIAL ESTATE
38
A
B
C
D
WELL LANE
Roughmoor
Kennels
22
39
WESTFIELD
CORONATION RD.
THOMAS
LITTLEFIELDS
SCHOOL LA.
CHURCH ST.
Sch.
The Square
Hillend Farm
59
HIGH STREET
NORTH VIEW DR.
BANWELL
Banwell
HILL PATH
ROCKY LA.
The Caves
Caves
Banwell Monument
BANWELL HILL
Sewage Works
1
M5 MOTORWAY
Whitley Head
Warren Cottage
BRIDEWELL LANE
BRIDEWELL LA.
BS29
Winthill House
WINTHILL
Winthill Farm
Winfield
CHRISTON ROAD
2
M5
58
Yarberry Farm
Yarberry
River Yeo
Barleycombe
3
The Beeches
29
Manor Farm
FLAGSTAFF RD.
BANWELL ROAD
4
CHRISTON RD.
Christon
Axbridge
BS26
57
Lox Yeo
NORTH SOMERSET
SEDGEMOOR
5
M5
Laurel Farm
Home Farm
Barton Farm
Lime Trees
Rose Farm
Nut Tree Farm
Barton Camp
Barton
BARTON ROAD
Long Acre
6
Barton Rocks
Barton Hill
The Paddock
56
A
B
C
D
38
39
The Lodge
Crook Peak
Compton Hill
Coombe Bungalow
Coombe Cottage

23
41
42
E
F
G
H
A368
ST.
Banwell Plain
Depot
Banwell Wood
QUARRY
RD.
59
SOUTH CROFT
SOUTH HILL
Broadleaze Farm
1
Towerhead
SMALL DOWN END
Sandford Batch
SANDFORD ROAD
WIMBLESTONE
COPSE END
BROADLEAZE WY.
A371
BANWELL HILL ROAD
Banwell Castle
Castle Cottages
Nursery
Rhodyate Lodge
RHODYATE
Rhodyate Farm
THE RHODYATE
ILEX LA.
SHIPHAM LANE
Cemetery
RAILWAY WALK
THE GROVE
Sloughpit Farm
2
EVERGREEN CL.
HOMEFIELD CL.
MOORHAM RD.
ASH CL.
PLUM TREE CL.
58
BIGNELL CL.
HOMESTEAD WY.
ROAD
Bowl. Grn.
Winscombe
Mooseheart
KNAPPS CL.
KNAPPS DR.
ROCKERIES DR.
Rob-Lynne Ct.
NIPPORS WY.
3
WOODBOROUGH RD.
Mendip Lodge
HILLFIELDS WY.
Water Works
MILL LANE
Max Mills Farm
Nut Tree Farm
66
73
WOODBOROUGH ROAD
WINSCOMBE
Dunster Ct.
THE GRN.
32
APPLE TREE DR.
SOUTHMEAD
SIDCOT
ASHLEY CL.
WOODBOROUGH CR.
THE LYNCH
BARBON CL.
THE CHESTNUTS
Max House Farm
BS25
THE LYNCH
LYNCH CR.
4
LYNCH MEAD
YADLEY CL.
YADLEY WAY
Playing F
Football Ground
Club Ho.
57
Memorial Rec. Grd.
ROAD
PARSONS WAY
Willow Farm
Barton Grange
CHURCH ROAD
The Square
Barton Kennels
Laurel Farm
EASTWELL LA.
CHURCH LA.
WINSCOMBE HILL
Winscombe Court
EASTWELL
SOUTHLEAZE
FULLERS LANE
5
YADLEY LANE
Broad Knoll
Coombe Wood
DROVE
BARTON DROVE
Church Knoll
Old Quarry Farm
Saw Mill
WINSCOMBE
6
Winscombe Hill
Reservoir (Covered)
The Hall
HILL
Hill Farm
156
KING'S WOOD

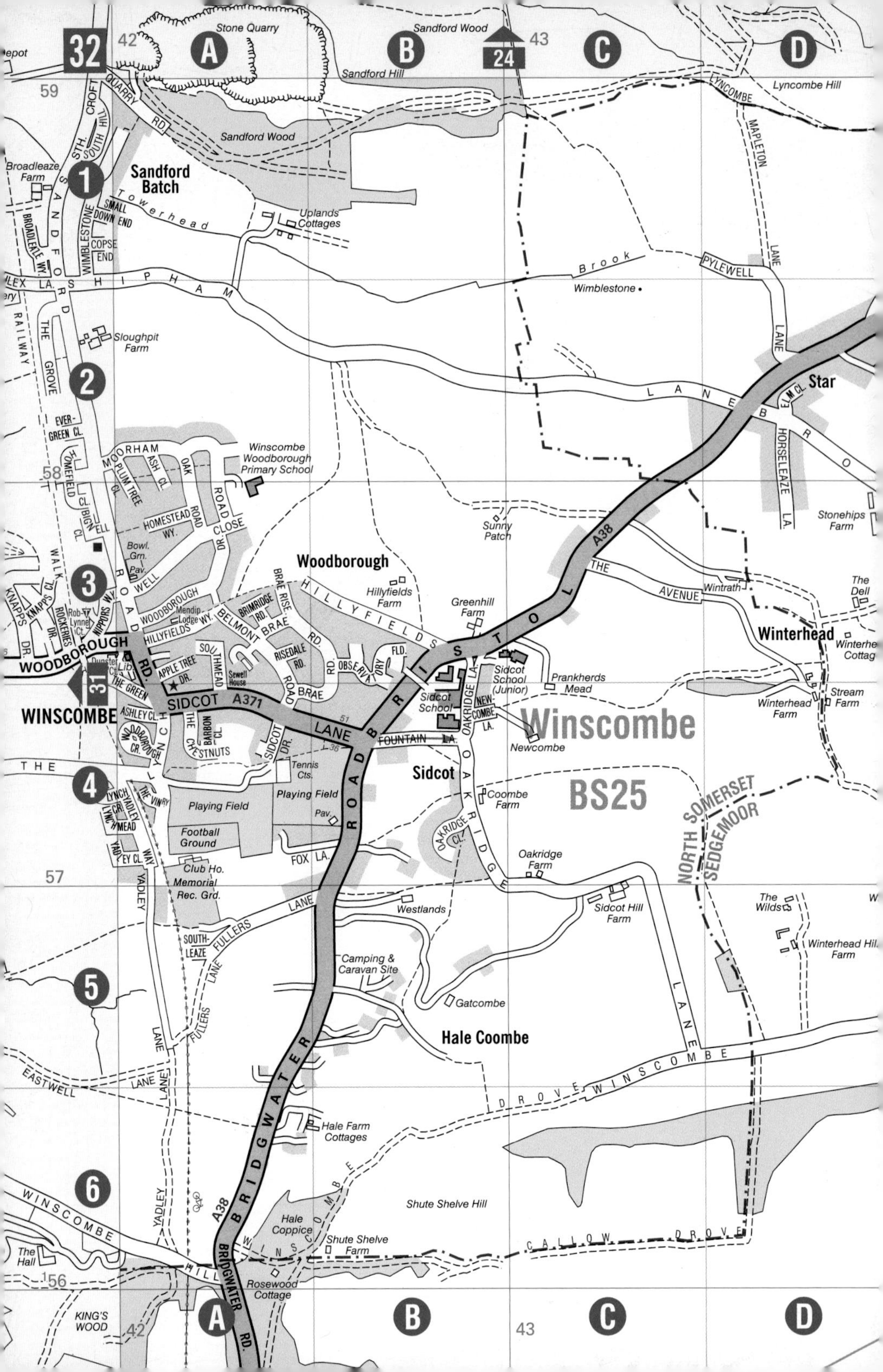

Stone Quarry
Sandford Wood
24
Sandford Hill
Sandford Wood
Lyncombe Hill
Sandford Batch
Broadleaze Farm
Uplands Cottages
Towerhead
Brook
Wimblestone
Sloughpit Farm
SHIPHAM
Star
Winscombe Woodborough Primary School
Sunny Patch
Stonehips Farm
Woodborough
Hillyfields Farm
Greenhill Farm
The Dell
Winterhead
Winterhead Cottage
Sidcot School (Junior)
Prankherds Mead
Sidcot School
Stream Farm
Winterhead Farm
WINSCOMBE
Winscombe
Newcombe
Sidcot
BS25
Coombe Farm
NORTH SOMERSET
SEDGEMOOR
Tennis Cts.
Playing Field
Playing Field
Football Ground
Club Ho.
Memorial Rec. Grd.
Oakridge Farm
Westlands
Sidcot Hill Farm
The Wilds
Winterhead Hill Farm
Camping & Caravan Site
Gatcombe
Hale Coombe
Hale Farm Cottages
Shute Shelve Hill
Hale Coppice
Shute Shelve Farm
The Hall
Rosewood Cottage
KING'S WOOD
A38
A371
BRISTOL ROAD
BRIDGWATER ROAD
SIDCOT LANE
WOODBOROUGH RD.
WINSCOMBE DROVE
CALLOW DROVE
FULLERS LANE
YADLEY LANE
EASTWELL LANE
PYLEWELL LANE
LYNCOMBE
MAPLETON LANE
THE AVENUE
FOX LA.
FOUNTAIN LA.
OAKRIDGE
HILLYFIELDS
BROAD LANE

31

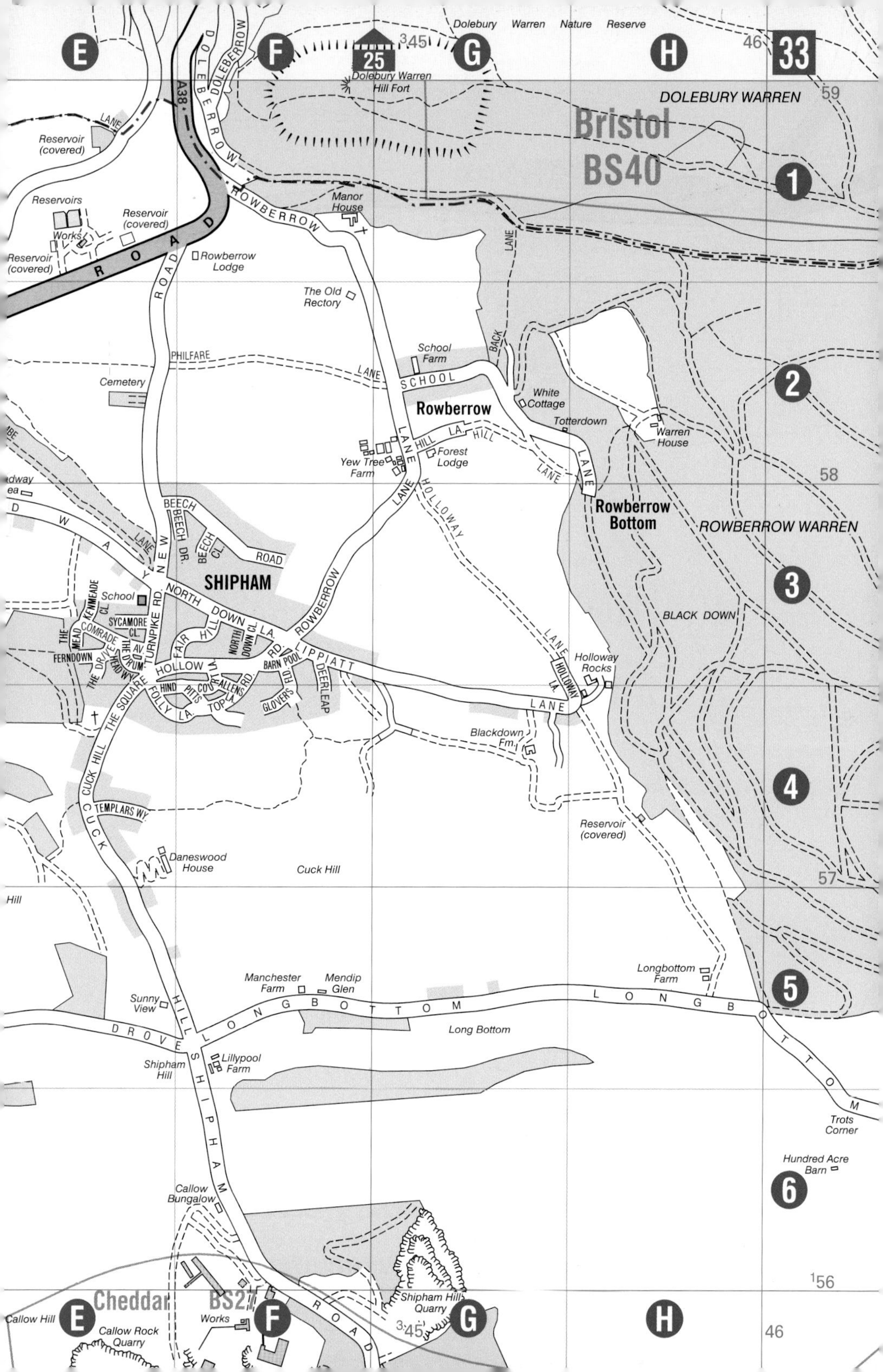
Dolebury Warren Nature Reserve
25
Dolebury Warren Hill Fort
DOLEBURY WARREN
Bristol
BS40
DOLEBERROW
A38
ROAD
Reservoir (covered)
Reservoirs
Works
Manor House
ROWBERROW
Rowberrow Lodge
The Old Rectory
School Farm
PHILFARE
Cemetery
SCHOOL LANE
BACK LANE
White Cottage
Totterdown
Warren House
Rowberrow
HILL LA.
Yew Tree Farm
Forest Lodge
Rowberrow Bottom
ROWBERROW WARREN
HOLLOWAY
BEECH ROAD
BEECH DR.
BEECH CL.
NEW LANE
SHIPHAM
School
KENMEADE CL.
SYCAMORE CL.
COMRADE AV.
THE MEAD
FERNDOWN
THE DRIVE
HEADWY.
THE DRUM
TURNPIKE RD.
NORTH DOWN LA.
NORTH DOWN CL.
FAIR HILL
HOLLOW RD.
BARN POOL
LIPPIATT LANE
DEERLEAP
GLOVERS FLD.
HIND PITS
COURT LA.
ALLENS RD.
TOP LA.
FOLLY LA.
THE SQUARE
BLACK DOWN
Holloway Rocks
HOLLOWAY LA.
Blackdown Fm.
CUCK HILL
TEMPLARS WY.
Daneswood House
Cuck Hill
Reservoir (covered)
Hill
Longbottom Farm
Manchester Farm
Mendip Glen
Sunny View
LONGBOTTOM
DROVE
Long Bottom
Shipham Hill
Lillypool Farm
SHIPHAM
Trots Corner
Hundred Acre Barn
Callow Bungalow
Shipham Hill Quarry
Cheddar
BS27
Callow Hill
Works
Callow Rock Quarry
ROAD
E
F
G
H
1
2
3
4
5
6
345
46
59
58
57
156

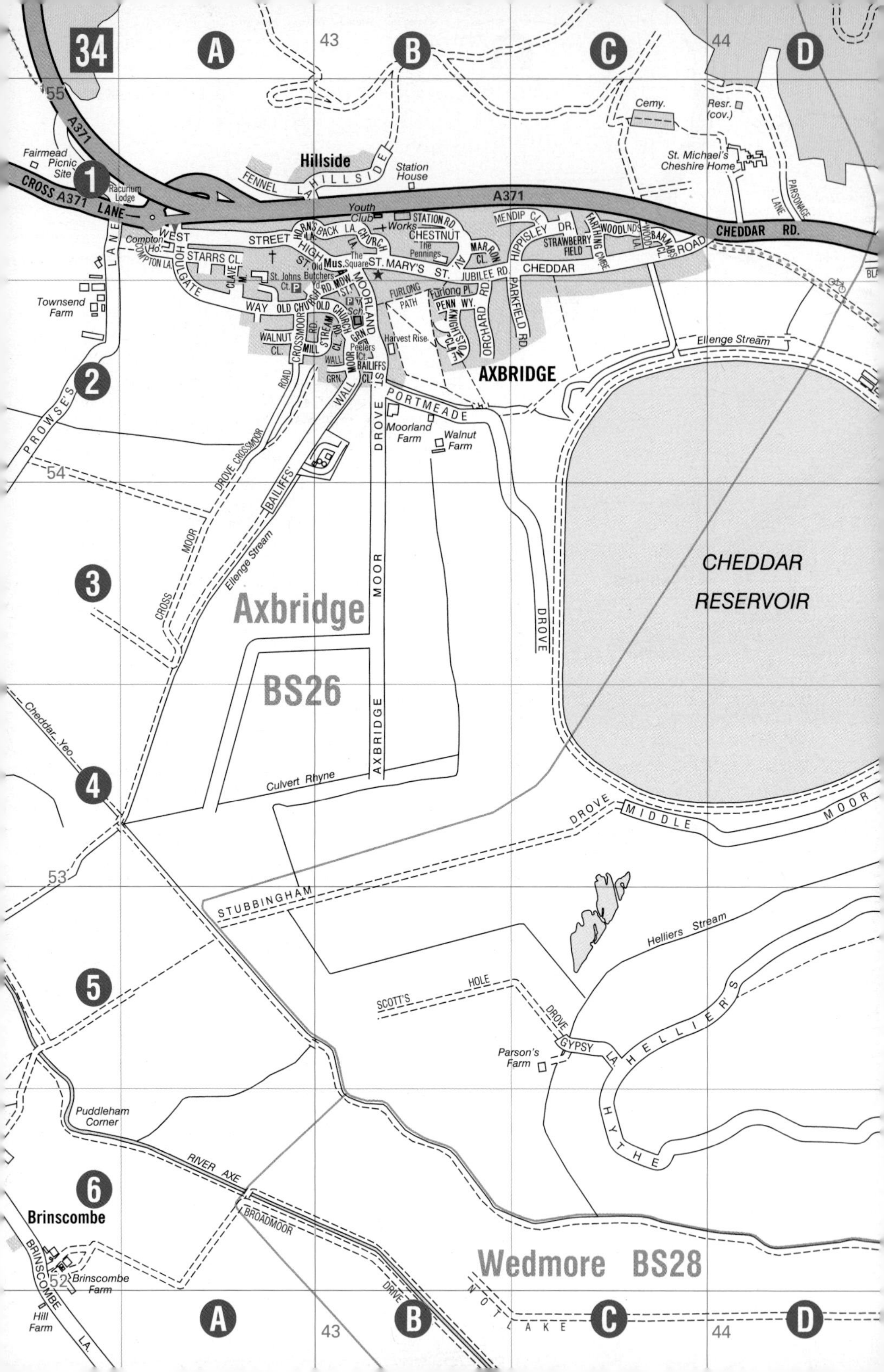
A
B
C
D
43
44
55
54
53
52
1
2
3
4
5
6
A371
Fairmead Picnic Site
Racurium Lodge
CROSS A371 LANE
Hillside
FENNEL LA.
HILLSIDE
Station House
A371
Cemy.
Resr. (cov.)
St. Michael's Cheshire Home
PARSONAGE LANE
CHEDDAR RD.
Youth Club
Works
STATION RD.
CHESTNUT
The Pennings
MENDIP CL.
HIPPISLEY DR.
STRAWBERRY FIELD
FARTHING CMBE.
WOODLNDS
WOOD LA.
BARNABAS CL.
ROAD
MARRON CL.
Compton Ho.
COMPTON LA.
WEST
STREET
HORN'S LA.
BACK LA.
CHURCH LA.
HIGH ST.
Mus.
The Square
ST. MARY'S ST.
JUBILEE RD.
CHEDDAR
HOULGATE WAY
STARRS CL.
CLAVE M.
St. Johns Ct.
Old Butchers Yd.
RD. MDW.
MOORLAND ST.
Sch.
OLD CHURCH
STREAM
CHURCH RD. CL.
Townsend Farm
WALNUT CL.
CROSSMOOR RD.
MILL
Peelers Ct.
WALL GRN.
MOOR GRN.
BAILIFFS CL.
BAILIFFS' WALL
FURLONG PATH
Furlong Pl.
PENN WY.
KNIGHTSTONE CL.
ORCHARD RD.
PARKFIELD RD.
Harvest Rise
AXBRIDGE
Ellenge Stream
PORTMEADE
Moorland Farm
Walnut Farm
PROWSE'S LANE
CROSSMOOR DROVE
Ellenge Stream
CROSS MOOR
Axbridge
BS26
MOOR DROVE
AXBRIDGE
DROVE
CHEDDAR RESERVOIR
Cheddar Yeo
Culvert Rhyne
MIDDLE MOOR DROVE
STUBBINGHAM
Helliers Stream
SCOTT'S HOLE DROVE
GYPSY LA.
Parson's Farm
HELLIER'S HYTHE
Puddleham Corner
RIVER AXE
BROADMOOR DRIVE
Brinscombe
Brinscombe Farm
BRINSCOMBE LA.
Hill Farm
Wedmore BS28
NOTLAKE

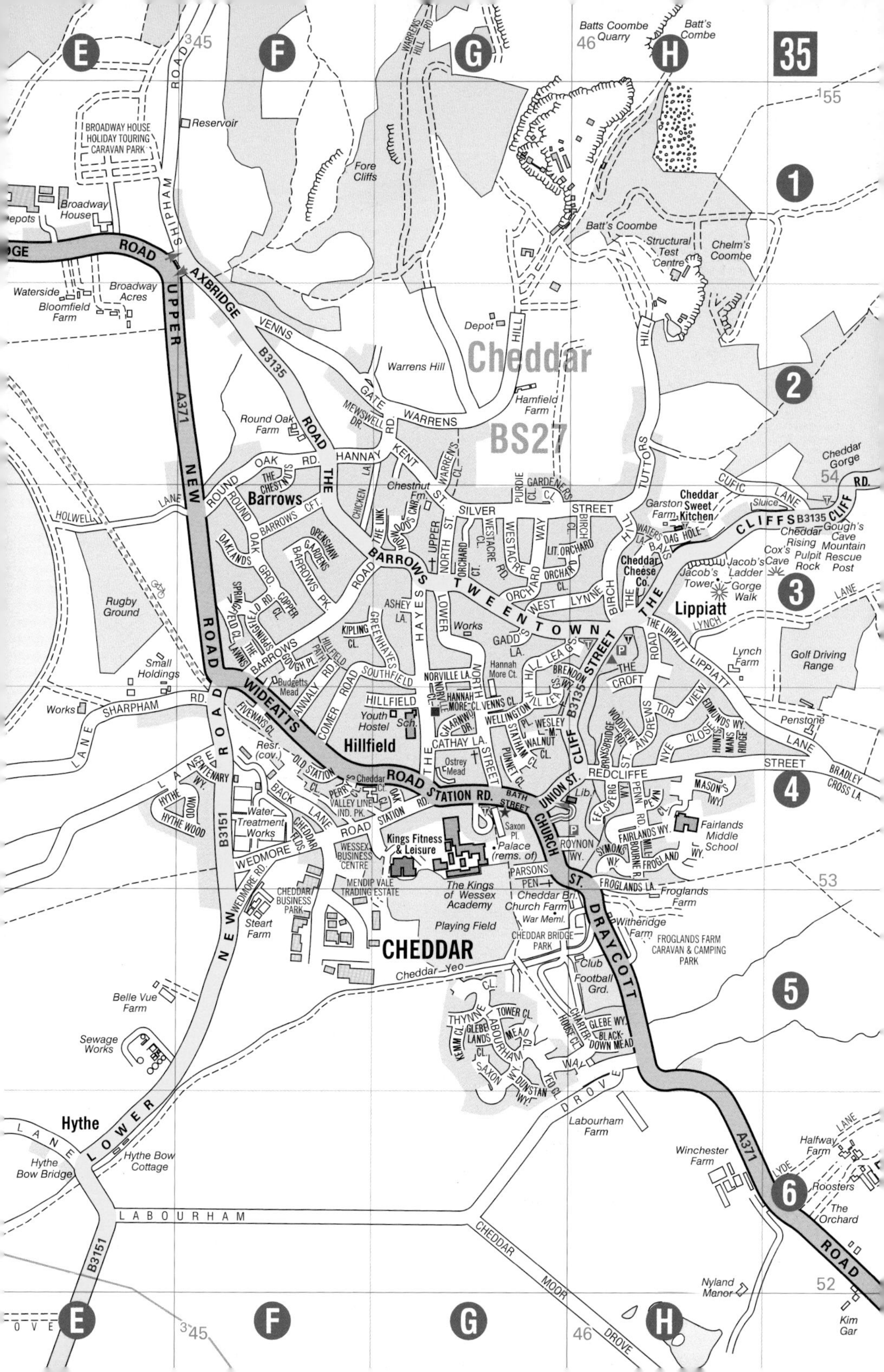
E
F
G
H
345
46
Batts Coombe Quarry
Batt's Combe
55
54
53
52
1
2
3
4
5
6
BROADWAY HOUSE HOLIDAY TOURING CARAVAN PARK
Reservoir
SHIPHAM ROAD
WARRENS HILL RD.
Fore Cliffs
Broadway House
Depots
ROAD
Waterside
Bloomfield Farm
Broadway Acres
Batt's Coombe
Structural Test Centre
Chelm's Coombe
AXBRIDGE
VENNS
B3135
UPPER
A371
NEW
Depot
HILL
Cheddar
Warrens Hill
GATE
Hamfield Farm
Round Oak Farm
MEWSWELL DR.
WARRENS
BS27
ROAD
THE
HANNAY
RD.
KENT
WARREN'S CL.
TUTTORS
HILL
Cheddar Gorge
OAK RD.
THE CHESTNUTS
ROUND
Barrows
CHICKEN LA.
Chestnut Fm.
PURDIE CL.
GARDENERS CL.
CUFIC LANE
RD.
LANE
HOLWELL
BARROWS CFT.
THE LINK
WOOD'S CNR.
SILVER STREET
Garston Farm
Cheddar Sweet Kitchen
Sluice
B3135 CLIFF
CLIFFS
Gough's Cave
Cheddar Rising
Mountain Rescue Post
Cox's Cave
Pulpit Rock
OAKLANDS
OAK GRO.
OPENSHAW GARDENS
BARROWS PK.
UPPER NORTH ST.
ORCHARD CT.
WESTACRE CL.
WESTACRE RD.
WAY
BIRCH CL.
LIT. ORCHARD
WATERS LA.
BAYS
DAG HOLE
Jacob's Ladder
Jacob's Tower
Gorge Walk
Cheddar Cheese Co.
BARROWS
TWEENTOWN
ORCHARD
ORCHARD CL.
WEST LYNNE
BIRCH
THE
Lippiatt
LANE
LYNCH
Rugby Ground
SPRING FIELD RD.
SPRINGFIELD CL.
LAWNS
COPPER CL.
ASHEY LA.
GREENHAYES
HAYES
LOWER
Works
GADD'S LA.
HILL LEA GS.
STREET
THE LIPPIATT
LIPPIATT
Lynch Farm
Golf Driving Range
KIPLING CL.
HILLFIELD PATH
GOUGH PL.
Small Holdings
Budgetts Mead
ANNALY RD.
SOUTHFIELD
Hannah More Ct.
NORTH
BRENDON WY.
THE CROFT
ROAD
Works
SHARPHAM RD.
WIDEATTS
COMER ROAD
HILLFIELD
NORVILLE LA.
NORVILLE CL.
HANNAH MORE CL.
VENNS CL.
HILL LEA GS.
B3135
TOR VIEW
EDMUNDS WY.
Penstone
LANE
FIVEWAYS CL.
Youth Hostel
Sch.
CHARNWOOD DR.
WELLINGTON PL.
WESLEY M.
CLIFF
WOODVIEW
ANDREWS
CLOSE
HUNTS
MANS RIDGE
NYE
Resr. (cov.)
OLD STATION CL.
Hillfield
CATHAY LA.
STATHAM CL.
WALNUT CL.
BRADSBRIDGE
ST.
Ostrey Mead
PUNNET CL.
REDCLIFFE STREET
BRADLEY CROSS LA.
CENTENARY WY.
HYTHE
WOOD
HYTHE WOOD
PERRY'S CL.
Cheddar Valley Line Ind. Pk.
OAK
ROAD STATION RD.
BATH STREET
UNION ST.
Lib.
FELSBERG WY.
PENN RD.
PENN CL.
MASON'S WY.
BACK LANE
STATION ROAD
Water Treatment Works
B3151
CHEDDAR FLDS.
Kings Fitness & Leisure
Saxon Pl.
Palace (rems. of)
CHURCH
ROYNON WY.
FAIRLANDS WY.
SYMONS WY.
BOURNE R.
MILL
FROGLAND
WY.
Fairlands Middle School
WEDMORE ROAD
WESSEX BUSINESS CENTRE
MENDIP VALE TRADING ESTATE
The Kings of Wessex Academy
PARSONS PEN
Cheddar Bri.
Church Farm
FROGLANDS LA.
Froglands Farm
WEDMORE RD.
CHEDDAR BUSINESS PARK
Steart Farm
Playing Field
War Meml.
CHEDDAR BRIDGE PARK
ST.
DRAYCOTT
Witheridge Farm
FROGLANDS FARM CARAVAN & CAMPING PARK
CHEDDAR
Cheddar Yeo
Club
Football Grd.
NEW
Belle Vue Farm
CL.
THYNNE CL.
GLEBE LANDS
TOWER CL.
LABOURHAM
MEAD CL.
KEMM CL.
CHARTER HOUSE CL.
GLEBE WY.
BLACK-DOWN MEAD
Sewage Works
SAXON WY.
DUNSTAN WY.
YEO CL.
WAY
DROVE
Labourham Farm
Hythe
LOWER
LANE
Hythe Bow Bridge
Hythe Bow Cottage
Winchester Farm
A371
Halfway Farm
LANE
LYDE
Roosters
The Orchard
LABOURHAM
CHEDDAR MOOR DROVE
ROAD
B3151
Nyland Manor
Kim Gar
DROVE

A
B
C
D
1
2
3
4
5
6
330
31
52
51
150
49
BERROW
Berrow C of E Prim. School
ROSETREE PADDOCK
RUGOSA DR.
BARTON RD.
FAIRWAY CL.
ROSENEATH AV.
SANDHILLS DR.
OLD COTE DR.
Rec. Grd.
BERROW RD.
Faircott Farm
Mulberry Centre
B3140
Rhyne
Erika Cottage
Kennels
Greenways
Chillpark
ROAD HAM
BRENT ROAD
BERROW ROAD
MARTIN'S CL.
BLYTHE WY.
ASH TREE CR.
ASH TREE ROAD
ASH TREE PL.
Ashcombe Ho.
OAK TREE PL.
LINKS CL.
TIDBALL RD.
NAISH RD.
LINKS GDNS.
BURNHAM & BERROW GOLF COURSE
SAXONDALE AVENUE
GOLF LINKS ROAD
NEWTON CL.
BRAITHWAITE PL.
Pitland
THE DRIVE
The Orchids
REGENCY CL.
ST. CHRISTOPHER'S WAY
Club House
EDITH CL.
PATRICIA CL.
THE RETREAT CARAVAN PARK
COLERIDGE GDNS.
WORDSWORTH CL.
SHELLEY DRIVE
SHELLEY CL.
BRIGHTSTOWE RD.
Applewithy Rhyne
BRENT BROAD
Brent Broad Farm
MAGPIE WAY
FINCHES
NIGHTINGALE CL.
BRAMBLES ROAD
WINDSOR CL.
HILLSBOROUGH GDNS.
PEMBROKE CL.
BALMORAL DR.
CAERNARVON WAY
CONWAY
CADBURY CL.
NUNNEY CL.
WARWICK GDS.
CONWAY CRES.
BURNHAM TOURING PARK
Club House
Sports Ground
ST. ANN'S DR.
GORE RD.
MOUNT BATTEN CL.
TRINITY CL.
PIZEY AV.
TRINITY RI.
STODDEN'S ROAD
PLAYER'S LANE
MARLBOROUGH CT.
GROVE
The Towans
The Colony
Treasure Ct.
The Gro. M.
Ten. Cts.
GARDENHURST
Burnham-on-Sea
Stoddens Farm
CROOKE
STODDEN'S WLK.
KNOLL VW.
STONELEIGH CLOSE
CRESWICK WY.
EASTLEIGH CL.
ALLANDALE RD.
Homelane Ho.
Beaufort Ct.
RECTORY DRIVE
GROVE RD.
HERBERT RD.
Allandale Ct.
B3140
PARNELL WAY
HURST CL.
GARDEN
RECTORY LAWN
WESTFIELD
WESTMERE PL.
RECTORY CRES.
Hunt's Pond
MARWOOD CL.
ATYEO CL.
HARBOURNE CL.
LEA ROAD
PALMERS
STODDEN'S RD.
STODDEN'S
Middle Burnham
POPLAR RD.
Belfield Ct.
CHARLESTONE RD.
Caravan Park
SPAXTON CL.
SIDMOUTH CL.
SOUTHERN
MEADOWCROFT DR.
WEDMORE CL.
BATHURST
Atlanta Key
MADDOCKS SLADE
Blencathara Ct.
SEAVIEW RD.
WESTFIELD RD.
TA8
CHEDDAR CL.
AXBRIDGE CL.
ENMORE CL.
BUCKLAND CL.
WAY
CORSHAM DR.
FROBISHER
HALL TER.
Spts. Acad.
Comm. Cen.
MYRTLE DR.
Steart Ct.
Churchlands Ct.
Playgrd.
Putt. Grn.
Ten. Cts.
CHESTER CL.
Cemetery
Manor Gdns.
ROAD
ST. MARK'S
SALVIN CL.
Sch.
Play Area
WINCHESTER RD.
BARRINGTON CL.
WILTON
AVEBURY CL.
EXBURY
RAMSAY
DYRHAM
Offs.
Bowls Grn.
Pav.
ST. JOHN'S RD.
ST. ANDREW'S RD.
ST. PAUL'S RD.
ST. MARY'S RD.
WELLS CL.
GLOUCESTER RD.
EXETER CL.
HAWLEY RD.
TRURO CL.
BURNETT CL.
POWLEY CL.
VINCENT
HOWARD CL.
BURNHAM-ON-SEA
Vicarage Ct.
VICARAGE ST.
VICTORIA ST.
MANOR RD.
Library
MIU
HOSP.
ST. MICHAEL'S RD.
ST. LUKE'S CL.
ST. PETER'S RD.
SALISBURY RD.
WINCHESTER
BERFD
HAWKINS GONS.
GRENVILLE
BEATTY WY.
LOVE
Cin.
Kinver Ter.
REGENT ST.
GEORGE
CHAPEL
PRINCESS ST.
Crown Gs.
RAVENS
OXFORD ST.
B3139
KINGSWAY RD.
Junior Sch.
Play. Fld.
WESTMANS TRADING ESTATE
RALEIGH
FRASER CL.
DEWAR CL.
CUNNINGHAM
MAD. DEN CLO.
LOUVIGNE CL.
Burnham
Pav.
College Ct.
COLLEGE ST.
HIGH STREET
ADAM
CROSS
DUNSTAN RD.
ROSEWOOD CLOSE
QUANTOCK CL.
MENDIP WY.
121
LANE
Supermarket
Sorting Off.
SHEARN
STREET
JAYCROFT RD.
ASHCOTT PL.
FRANK FOLEY PARKWAY
Burnham Level
Play. Fld.
Elizabeth Ct.
COTTAGE RW.
HAM LANE
SOUTH ST.
Sunny Lawns
BURNHAM SHOP. CEN.
TECHNICAL
JUBILEE
ABINGDON
STREET
ABBOTS
Primary
MONKS
BONIFACE
ROSEWOOD
ASHCOTT CL.
WAY
NOEL COWARD CL.
SHAW
STOPPARD
THE

38

E
F
G
H
33
34
52
51
50
49
1
2
3
4
5
6
North Grove Farm
WICK LANE
MIDDLE STREET
B3140
BURTON ROW
Grove Farm
Holly Tree Farm
Reservoirs (covered)
Ham Farm
Ham
Works
STATION ROAD
ROAD
Brent Corner
West Croft Farm
STH. BRENT CL.
Yonder Hill
LANE
Woodbine Farm
Slade Farm
Withies
Crooked Lane Bridge
CROOKED LANE
Musk Farm
Quantock View
Manor Farm
Giles Cottage
Giles's Copse
Ball Copse
Ball Copse Hall
Woodlands
Shipton's Copse
Brent Knoll
HILL LANE
Nightingale Farm
CHURCH LANE
LAUREL AV.
Brent Knoll
Vic.
Village Green
THE WILLOWS
Ten. Ct.
CHURCH LA.
CEDAR CL.
The Shrubbery
Manor House
MANOR RIDE
EAST RIDE
BRENT CL.
COOMBE SIDE
Brent Knoll C of E Primary Sch.
B3140
BATTLEBOROUGH LA.
BATTLEBOROUGH LANE
PORTLAND PL.
Highbridge
TA9
BRENT STREET
Brent Knoll
White Cross Farm
HARP RD.
ROAD
A38
M5
M5 MOTORWAY
Junc. 22
Ashland Farm
Depot
EDITHMEAD LANE
Edithmead Bridge
Inner Farm
Edithmead Farm
HOME FARM HOLIDAY PARK & COUNTRY PARK
Homestead
Rhyne
LANE
Edithmead
Chestnut Farm
Burnham
EDITHMEAD
Rhyne
BRISTOL
WINDMILL CL.
EDITHMEAD PARK
Rose Cottage
Bro LA.
House
39

A
B
C
D
1
2
3
4
5
6
330
31
49
48
47
146
36
BURNHAM-ON-SEA
Burnham-on-Sea
TA8
Bridgwater Bay
RIVER PARRETT
LOVE LANE
B3140
Supermarket
Burnham Le
BOARD'S
THE FRANK FOLEY PARKWAY
OXFORD STREET
B3139
HIGHBRIDGE ROAD
BURNHAM ROAD
Pav.
College Ct.
CHAPL.
COLL-EGE
JOHN ST.
CROSS
ADAM
COTTAGE
HAM
SMITH ST.
Sunny Lawns
BURNHAM SHOP. CEN.
HIGH ST.
TECHNICAL ST.
ABINGDON
JUBILEE ST.
HUDSON ST.
SHEARN LA.
STREET
DUNSTAN RD.
KINGSW
Play. Fld.
QUANTOCK RD.
JAYCROFT RD.
CLOISTERS CFT.
PRIORY
ABBOTS
MONKS WY.
MENDIP WY.
Elizabeth Ct.
FRIARS WY.
Play. Fld.
ASHCOTT PL.
Primary Sch.
BONIFACE WK.
BISHOP'S PATH
DEACON WY.
GDNS.
ROSEWOOD AVENUE
ROSEWOOD DR.
ASHCOTT CL.
ASHCOTT DRIVE
ROSE CL.
Briar Ct.
BRIAR CT.
ASHCOTT
WAY
OLIVIER CL.
COWARD RD.
NOEL
SHAW PTH.
BARRIE WY.
TRAVERS'
STOPPARD
RATTIGAN
ARCHER DR.
OSBORNE WLK.
PINTER CL.
WILDE CL.
BEN JONSON
BEN
GIELGUD CL.
TRAVERS
WAY
SHERIDAN RD.
WOOD FIELD
ALDWYCH CL.
PRIEST LEY WAY
COOKSON CL.
THORNDIKE WY.
MARITIME
ESPLANADE
PIER ST.
MARINE
Superstore
LYNTON RD.
ETON RD.
ASHLEY AV.
Saints Ct.
SUTHERLAND AV.
KILLARNEY
WORSTON
STEART DR.
STEART GS.
STEART CL.
STEART AVENUE
TATAM CL.
BIRCH LAWN
MAPLE DR.
MARGARET CR.
SYCAMORE CL.
MAPLE DRIVE
Knightstone Ct.
Holts Ho.
Quantock Ct.
Tennis Courts
Pitch & Putt Course
HOLM CL.
DR.
BRUE CR.
LUNDY
SEVERN GRO.
ATLANTIC CRES.
LUNDY DR.
CHANNEL CT.
BAY VW. GS.
BROADHURST GARDENS
THORNE PK.
CHANNING CL.
Willis Ct.
CHURCHILL CL.
Worston Rhyne
Playing Fields
Pav.
CASS'S CL.
LANE
WORSTON
HOOPER CL.
WALLACE
HATCHER CL.
WELLS
LAWRENCE CL.
STOWE R.
BEALE WY.
HEAL CL.
RD.
Depot
King Alfred Sports Cen.
Playing Field
The King Alfred School
SOUTH
Holiday Camp
Holiday Camp
Tennis Courts
BURNHAM-ON-SEA HOLIDAY VILLAGE
DRIVE
HIGHBURN CL.
APEX DRIVE
Holimarine
Apex Leisure & Wildlife Park
BRUE PILL
PARSONS RD.
DUNBAR CL.
NORTH AV.
NORTH
WEST AV.
QUEENS SQ.
SOUTH AV.
EAST AV.
THREE YARDS CT.
SANDY CT.
HUISH CL.
Huish
AVENUE
ROAD
B3139
OLDWAY PL.
JASMINE CL.
PEPPERALL
OLDWAY
MEADOW CL.
SANDACRE RES. PK.
OLD BURNHAM RD.
PADDOCK
FIELD WY.
ELDER CL.
LOBLIA CL.
MARCO
GULLIFORD CL.
TROWBRIDGE CL.
WALLARD PL.
TRES-GELLIS
TALBOT CL.
MORLAND
KILN DR.
MORLANDS IND. PARK
Rhyne
PEARCE DR.
Play. Fld.
Sch.
News
CORONATION
Newtown Lake
Victoria Pl.
POPLAR EST.
POPLAR
JOHN ST.
CUTHBERT ST.
NEWTOWN R.
TYLER WY.
Sewage Works
Depot
TASKER CL.
SMITH WY.
SPARKS WY.
WILLET CL.
KIMBER CL.
SCOTT RD.
Riverbed Ho.
Jubilee Gds.
CLYCE
ROAD
New Clyce Bri.
HIGHBRIDGE QUAY
Vardy Ct.
Charlotte Ct.
Alstone Hall
MEADOW VW.
Common Farm
PREMIER BUSINESS PARK
HUNTSPILL ROAD
ALSTONE
Alstone
ADAMS CL.
ROAD
Alstone Court Farm
ALSTONE LANE
ALSTONE GS.
MAIN ROAD
A38
Sewage Works
LEEKBEDS
Westfield
MIDDLE FIELD LANE
Rhyne LANE
Mulberry House Farm
Maundril's Farm
SMURL LA.
North Rhyne
West Huntspill Prim. Sch.
Playing Field
Pav.
Barberry House
NEW
Huntspill
LANGLANDS LA.
SHEPHERD'S
LANE
Greenwood Farm
GREENWOOD CL.
CHURCH
RD.
Plymor Hill Farm

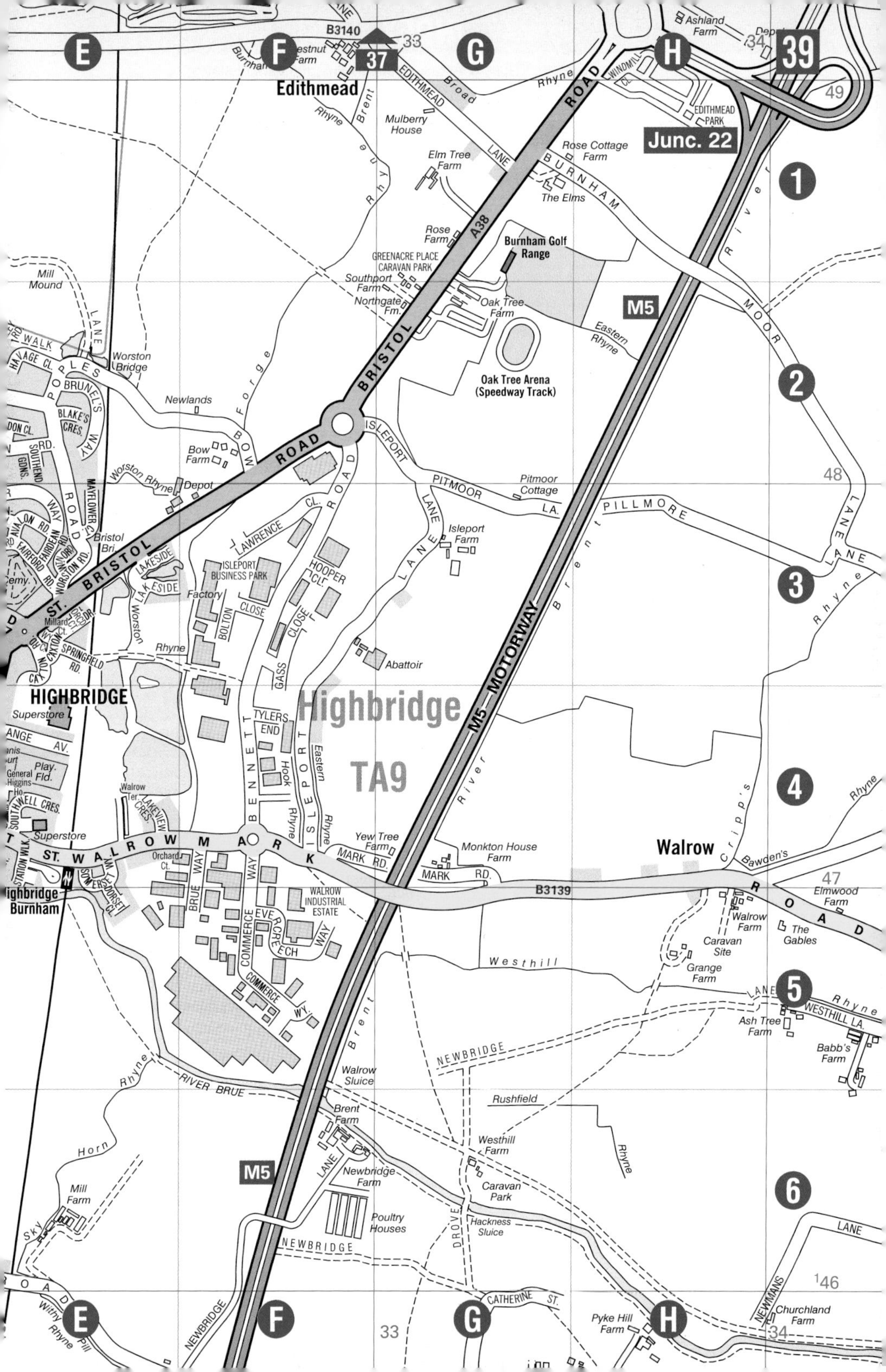
39
37
E
F
G
H
1
2
3
4
5
6
B3140
33
34
49
48
47
46
Ashland Farm
Depot
Edithmead
EDITHMEAD LANE
Broad Rhyne
Brent Rhyne
Mulberry House
WINDMILL CL.
EDITHMEAD PARK
Junc. 22
Rose Cottage Farm
Elm Tree Farm
BURNHAM MOOR LANE
The Elms
River Brent
Rose Farm
A38
BRISTOL ROAD
Burnham Golf Range
GREENACRE PLACE CARAVAN PARK
Southport Farm
Northgate Fm.
Oak Tree Farm
M5
Eastern Rhyne
Mill Mound
Oak Tree Arena (Speedway Track)
WALK
HAVAGE CL.
POPLES LANE
Worston Bridge
BRUNEL'S WAY
BLAKE'S CRES.
Newlands
Forge
DON CL.
SOUTHEND RD.
GDNS.
ISLEPORT ROAD
Bow Farm
Worston Rhyne
Depot
MAYFLOWER CT.
PITMOOR LA.
Pitmoor Cottage
PILLMORE LANE
AVALON RD.
FAIRDEAN RD.
FAIRFORD RD.
WORSTON RD.
Bristol Bri.
LAWRENCE CL.
Isleport Farm
LAKESIDE
ISLEPORT BUSINESS PARK
HOOPER CL.
ST. BRISTOL
Factory
BOLTON CLOSE
Worston
Millard Ct.
SPRINGFIELD RD.
Rhyne
GASS CLOSE
Abattoir
HIGHBRIDGE
Superstore
Highbridge
TYLERS END
ANGE AV.
Play. Fld.
General Higgins Ho.
Hook Rhyne
Eastern Rhyne
TA9
M5 MOTORWAY
SOUTHWELL CRES.
Walrow Ter.
LAKEVIEW CRES.
BENNETT WAY
Cripp's Rhyne
Superstore
Yew Tree Farm
Monkton House Farm
Walrow
ST. WALROW
MARK ROAD
MARK RD.
Bawden's
Orchard Ct.
STATION WLK.
SOMERSET M.
DORSET CL.
BRUE WAY
WALROW INDUSTRIAL ESTATE
B3139
Elmwood Farm
Highbridge Burnham
COMMERCE WAY
EVERCREECH WAY
Walrow Farm
The Gables
Caravan Site
Westhill
Grange Farm
WESTHILL LA.
Ash Tree Farm
Babb's Farm
NEWBRIDGE
Rhyne
RIVER BRUE
Walrow Sluice
Brent Farm
Rushfield
Horn
Westhill Farm
Newbridge Farm
Caravan Park
Mill Farm
Poultry Houses
Hackness Sluice
DROVE
LANE
Sky
ROAD
NEWBRIDGE
NEWMANS
CATHERINE ST.
Withy Rhyne
Pill
Pyke Hill Farm
Churchland Farm

INDEX

Including Streets, Places & Areas, Hospitals etc., Industrial Estates,
Selected Flats & Walkways, Stations and Selected Places of Interest.

HOW TO USE THIS INDEX

1. Each street name is followed by its Postcode District, then by its Locality abbreviation(s) and then by its map reference; e.g. **Accommodation Rd.** BS24: B'don . . . .6E **27** is in the BS24 Postcode District and the Bleadon Locality and is to be found in square 6E on page **27**. The page number is shown in bold type.

2. A strict alphabetical order is followed in which Av., Rd., St., etc. (though abbreviated) are read in full and as part of the street name; e.g. **Apple Tree Dr.** appears after **Appletree Ct.** but before **Appletree Gro.**

3. Streets and a selection of flats and walkways too small to be shown on the maps, appear in the index with the thoroughfare to which it is connected shown in brackets; e.g. **Albion Ter.** *BS27: Ched . . . .4G **35** (off Cliff St.)*

4. Addresses that are in more than one part are referred to as not continuous.

5. Places and areas are shown in the index in **BLUE TYPE** and the map reference is to the actual map square in which the town centre or area is located and not to the place name shown on the map; e.g. **AXBRIDGE 1B 34**

6. An example of a selected place of interest is **Helicpter Mus., The 4C 20**

7. An example of a station is **Highbridge & Burnham Station (Rail) 4E 39**

8. An example of a Hospital or Hospice is **BURNHAM-ON-SEA WAR MEMORIAL HOSPITAL 6B 36**

GENERAL ABBREVIATIONS

App. : Approach
Av. : Avenue
Bri. : Bridge
Bldgs. : Buildings
Bus. : Business
Cvn. : Caravan
C'way. : Causeway
Cen. : Centre
Chu. : Church
Circ. : Circle
Cir. : Circus
Cl. : Close
Comn. : Common
Cnr. : Corner
Cotts. : Cottages
Ct. : Court
Cres. : Crescent
Cft. : Croft
Dr. : Drive
E. : East
Est. : Estate
Fld. : Field
Flds. : Fields
Gdn. : Garden
Gdns. : Gardens
Ga. : Gate
Gt. : Great
Grn. : Green
Gro. : Grove
Hgts. : Heights
Ho. : House
Ind. : Industrial
Info. : Information
La. : Lane
Lit. : Little
Lwr. : Lower
Mnr. : Manor
Mans. : Mansions
Mdw. : Meadow
Mdws. : Meadows
M. : Mews
Mus. : Museum
Nth. : North
Pde. : Parade
Pk. : Park
Pl. : Place
Quad. : Quadrant
Res. : Residential
Ri. : Rise
Rd. : Road
Rdbt. : Roundabout
Shop. : Shopping
Sth. : South
Sq. : Square
Sta. : Station
St. : Street
Ter. : Terrace
Trad. : Trading
Up. : Upper
Va. : Vale
Vw. : View
Vs. : Villas
Wlk. : Walk
W. : West
Yd. : Yard

LOCALITY ABBREVIATIONS

Axb : **Axbridge**
Back : **Backwell**
Ban : **Banwell**
Bart : **Barton**
Berr : **Berrow**
B'don : **Bleadon**
Bour : **Bourton**
Brean : **Brean**
Bre K : **Brent Knoll**
Brin : **Brinscombe**
B'ley : **Brockley**
Bur S : **Burnham-on-Sea**
Ched : **Cheddar**
Chelv : **Chelvey**
Chri : **Christon**
C'hll : **Churchill**
C'ham : **Claverham**
C've : **Cleeve**
Clev : **Clevedon**
Clew : **Clewer**
Cong : **Congresbury**
Cross : **Cross**
E Brnt : **East Brent**
E Hunt : **East Huntspill**
E Rols : **East Rolstone**
Edith : **Edithmead**
Elbgh : **Elborough**
Hew : **Hewish**
High : **Highbridge**
Hut : **Hutton**
Iwood : **Iwood**
Kenn : **Kenn**
Kew : **Kewstoke**
L'frd : **Langford**
Lock : **Locking**
Lox : **Loxton**
Lym : **Lympsham**
Nail : **Nailsea**
Nye : **Nye**
Pux : **Puxton**
Redh : **Redhill**
Row : **Rowberrow**
St Geo : **St George's**
Sandf : **Sandford**
S'ham : **Shipham**
Star : **Star**
Tic : **Tickenham**
Udl : **Udley**
Uph : **Uphill**
Walt G : **Walton-in-Gordano**
W'fld : **Watchfield**
Webb : **Webbington**
W Hunt : **West Huntspill**
W Wick : **West Wick**
W Mare : **Weston-super-Mare**
W'ton V : **Weston Village**
Wick L : **Wick St Lawrence**
Wins : **Winscombe**
Wor : **Worle**
Wrax : **Wraxall**
Wrin : **Wrington**
Yat : **Yatton**

Bransby Way BS24: W'ton V . . .1E 21
Braysbridge BS27: Ched 4H 35
Breach La. BS48: Nail 4A 6
BREAN 6A 26
Brean Down Av.
BS23: W Mare 5D 18
Brean Down Rd.
TA8: Brean 1A 26
Brecon Vw. BS24: W Mare 2G 27
Bree Cl. BS22: Wor 3E 13
Brendon Av. BS23: W Mare 6F 11
Brendon Gdns. BS48: Nail 3E 7
Brendon Way BS27: Ched 3G 35
Brent Broad TA8: Bur S 3B 36
Brent Cl. BS24: W Mare 1H 27
TA9: Bre K 4H 37
BRENT KNOLL 3G 37
Brent Rd. TA8: Bur S 1A 36
TA9: Bre K 1A 36
Brent St. TA9: Bre K 2F 37
Briar Cl. BS48: Nail 2G 7
TA8: Bur S 1C 38
Briar Ct. TA8: Bur S 1C 38
Briar Mead BS49: Yat 4A 8
Briar Rd. BS24: Hut 6C 20
Briars, The BS48: Back 5F 7
Bridewell La.
BS24: Ban, Hut 3F 29
Bridge Farm Sq.
BS49: Cong 3D 14
Bridge Rd. BS23: W Mare 3F 19
BS24: B'don 5H 27
Bridgwater Ct.
BS24: W Mare 6G 19
Bridgwater Rd.
BS23: W Mare, B'don 6E 19
BS24: Lym 2F 27
BS25: Wins 6A 32
Brighton Rd. BS23: W Mare
. . . . .3E 19
Brightstowe Rd. TA8: Bur S . . .3A 36
Brimbleworth La.
BS22: St Geo 4G 13
Brimridge Rd. BS25: Wins 3A 32
BRINSCOMBE 6A 34
Brinscombe La. BS26: Brin 6A 34
BRINSEA 1E 25
Brinsea Batch BS49: Cong 6E 15
Brinsea La. BS49: Cong 1E 25
Brinsea Rd. BS49: Cong 4D 14
Bristol Rd.
BS22: St Geo, Wor 5F 13
BS24: W Wick 5F 13
BS25: C'hll 5F 25
BS25: Row, Star, Wins 4B 32
BS40: L'frd 5F 25
BS48: Wrax 1G 7
BS49: Cong 3D 14
TA9: Bre K, Edith, High . . .3E 39
Bristol Rd. Lwr.
BS23: W Mare 1D 18
Britannia Way BS21: Clev 6C 4
Broadcroft Av. BS49: C'ham 4F 9
Broadcroft Cl. BS49: C'ham 4F 9
Broadhurst Gdns.
TA8: Bur S 2B 38
Broadlands BS21: Clev 4F 5
Broadleaze Way
BS25: Wins 1H 31
Broadmoor Drove
BS28: Brin, Ched, Clew . . .6A 34
Broadoak Rd.
BS23: W Mare 6D 18
BS40: L'frd 4G 25
Broad St. BS40: Wrin 5B 16
BS49: Cong 3D 14
Broadway BS24: Lock 5H 21
BS24: W Mare 1F 27
BS25: S'ham, Star 2D 32
Broadway Ho. Holiday
Touring Caravan Pk.
BS27: Ched 1E 35
BROADWAY LODGE 2G 27
Brockley Cl. BS24: W Mare 2F 27
BS48: Nail 3D 6
Brockley Cres.
BS24: W Mare 2F 27
Brockley Way BS48: B'ley 3F 9
BS49: C'ham, C've 3F 9
(not continuous)
Brockway BS48: Nail 2F 7
Brompton Rd.
BS24: W Mare 1G 27
Bronte Cl. BS23: W Mare 5G 19
Brookfield Wlk. BS21: Clev 4F 5
Brooking Mdw. BS48: Nail 3D 6
Brookland Rd.
BS22: W Mare 2H 19
Brook Lodge Touring Cvn.
& Camping Pk.
BS40: Redh 6F 17
Brooklyn BS40: Wrin 5B 16
Broom Farm Cl. BS48: Nail 4E 7
Brownlow Rd.
BS23: W Mare 5E 19
Brue Cl. BS23: W Mare 4G 19
Brue Cres. TA8: Bur S 2B 38
Brue Way TA9: High 5F 39
Brunel Cl. BS24: W Mare 3F 27
Brunel Rd. BS48: Nail 3B 6
Brunel's Way TA9: High 2E 39
Brunel Way BS49: Yat 4A 8
Bruton BS24: W Mare 1G 27
Bruton Cl. BS48: Nail 4E 7
Bryant Gdns. BS21: Clev 6C 4
Buckingham Rd.
BS24: W Mare 1H 27
Buckland Cl. TA8: Bur S 5C 36
Buckland Grn. BS22: Wor 2E 13
Bucklands Batch BS48: Nail 4F 7
Bucklands Dr. BS48: Nail 4F 7
Bucklands End BS48: Nail 4F 7
Bucklands Gro. BS48: Nail 4F 7
Bucklands La. BS48: Nail 4F 7
Bucklands Vw. BS48: Nail 4G 7
Buckle Path BS24: W Wick 1G 21
Bude Cl. BS48: Nail 3G 7
Budgetts Mead BS27: Ched 3F 35
Bullhouse La. BS40: Wrin 4B 16
(not continuous)
Bunting Ct. BS22: Wor 6C 12
Burlington St.
BS23: W Mare 1E 19
Burnett Cl. TA8: Bur S 6C 36
Burnett Ind. Est. BS40: Wrin . . .6C 16
Burnham & Berrow Golf Course
. . . . .3A 36
Burnham Cl. BS24: W Mare . . .2F 27
Burnham Dr. BS24: W Mare . . .2F 27
Burnham Golf Range 1G 39
Burnham Moor La.
TA9: Edith, W'fld 1G 39
BURNHAM-ON-SEA 6A 36
Burnham-on-Sea Holiday Village
TA8: Bur S 2B 38
Burnham-on-Sea Swm
& Sports Academy 5A 36
Burnham-on-Sea Tourist Info. Cen.
. . . . .1A 38
BURNHAM-ON-SEA WAR MEMORIAL
HOSPITAL 6B 36
BURNHAM-ON-SEA WAR MEMORIAL
HOSPITAL MINOR
INJURIES UNIT (MIU) . . .6B 36
Burnham Rd. TA8: Bur S 2C 38
TA9: High 2C 38
Burnham Shop. Cen.
TA8: Bur S 1A 38
Burnham Touring Pk.
TA8: Bur S 4C 36
Burrington Av.
BS24: W Mare 2F 27
Burrington Cl.
BS24: W Mare 2F 27
BS48: Nail 3E 7
Burrows, The BS22: St Geo . . .4H 13
Burton Row TA9: Bre K 1F 37
Bury, The
BS24: Elbgh, Lock 6E 21
Butcombe BS24: W Mare 1G 27
Buttercup Cres. BS22: Wor 3E 13
Butterfield Pk. BS21: Clev 6C 4
Buttermere Rd.
BS23: W Mare 5G 19
BUTT'S BATCH 6B 16
Butt's Batch BS40: Wrin 6B 16
Butts Orchard BS40: Wrin 6B 16
Byefields BS21: Clev 6C 4
Bye Pass BS40: L'frd 4H 25
Byeways La. BS25: Sandf 5C 24
Byron Cl. BS24: Lock 5E 21
Byron Ct. BS23: W Mare 1F 19
Byron Rd. BS23: W Mare 5G 19
BS24: Lock 5E 21
Byways Pk. BS21: Clev 6C 4

C

Cabot Way BS22: Wor 4E 13
Cadbury Cl. TA8: Bur S 4C 36
Cadbury Farm Rd. BS49: Yat . . .6B 8
Cadbury Sq. BS49: Cong 4D 14
Cadogan Gro. BS48: Back 6H 7
Caernarvon Way TA8: Bur S . . .4B 36
Cairn Cl. BS48: Nail 3G 7
Caister Cl. BS23: W Mare 4F 19
Callow Drove BS25: Wins 6C 32
Calluna Cl. BS22: Wick L 2E 13
Camberley Wlk.
BS22: W Mare 1C 20
Cambridge Ct. BS40: Wrin 5B 16
Cambridge Gro. BS21: Clev 2D 4
Cambridge Pl.
BS23: W Mare 1D 18
Cambridge Rd. BS21: Clev 2D 4
Camden Ter. BS23: W Mare . . .2E 19
Campion Cl. BS22: W Mare . . .2B 20
Camplins BS21: Clev 6C 4
Camp Rd. BS23: W Mare 6B 10
Camp Rd. Nth.
BS23: W Mare 6B 10
Campus, The 1E 21
Camp Vw. BS48: Nail 2D 6
Canada Coombe BS24: Hut . . .1D 28
Canberra Cres. BS24: Lock 3F 21
Canberra Rd. BS23: W Mare . . .6F 19
Cannons Ga. BS21: Clev 6C 4
Canon's Wlk. BS22: Wor 5B 12
Canterbury Cl. BS22: Wor 3E 13
Capell Cl. BS22: W Mare 1H 19
Carberry Vw. BS24: W'ton V . . .2E 21
Cardigan Cres.
BS22: W Mare 1A 20
Carditch Drove BS49: Cong . . .1B 24
Carey's Cl. BS21: Clev 3F 5
Careys Way BS24: W'ton V 2C 20
Carice Gdns. BS21: Clev 6D 4
Carlton Mans. Nth.
BS23: W Mare 2D 18
(off Beach Rd.)
Carlton Mans. Sth.
BS23: W Mare 2D 18
(off Beach Rd.)
Carlton St. BS23: W Mare 2D 18
Caroline Pl. BS48: Back 6A 6
Carousel La. BS24: W'ton V . . .2C 20
Carpenter Cl.
BS23: W Mare 2G 19
Carre Gdns. BS22: Wor 3D 12
Cassis Cl. TA8: Bur S 2C 38
Castle Hill BS29: Ban 1E 31
Castlemead Shop. Cen.
BS22: Wor 2E 13
Castle Rd. BS21: Clev 1D 4
BS22: Wor 4C 12
Castle Vw. BS24: W'ton V 1D 20
Castle Vw. Rd. BS21: Clev 2D 4
Castlewood BS21: Clev 4F 5
Castlewood Cl. BS21: Clev 2D 4
Catemead BS21: Clev 6C 4
Cathay La. BS27: Ched 4G 35
Catherine St. TA9: E Hunt 6G 39
Caulfield Rd. BS22: Wor 3E 13
Causeway BS21: Nail, Tic 1B 6
BS48: Nail 2B 6
Causeway, The BS49: Cong . . .3D 14
BS49: Yat 6C 8
Causeway Vw. BS48: Nail 2C 6
Cavell Ct. BS21: Clev 6C 4
Caveners Ct. BS22: W Mare . . .6H 11
Caversham Dr. BS48: Nail 2G 7
Caxton Dr. TA9: High 3E 39
Caxton Rd. TA9: High 3E 39
Cecil Rd. BS23: W Mare 6E 11
Cedar Av. BS22: W Mare 6A 12
Cedar Cl. TA9: Bre K 3H 37
Cedar Ct. BS23: W Mare 6D 10
Cedarn Ct. BS22: Kew 3H 11
Cedar Way BS48: Nail 2G 7
Cedern Av. BS24: Elbgh 6G 21
Celtic Way BS24: B'don 3H 27
Centenary Way BS27: Ched 4F 35
Central Way BS21: Clev 6D 4
Centre, The BS23: W Mare 2E 19
Centre Dr. BS29: Ban 5A 22
Cerney Gdns. BS48: Nail 2G 7
Chaffins, The BS21: Clev 5E 5
Chalfont Rd. BS22: W Mare . . .1A 20
Challow Dr. BS22: W Mare 5H 11
Chamberlain Rd.
BS24: Lock 4G 21
Chancel Cl. BS48: Nail 4D 6
Chandos Ct. BS23: W Mare . . .3D 18
Channel Ct. TA8: Bur S 2B 38
Channel Hgts.
BS24: W Mare 2F 27
Channel Rd. BS21: Clev 1D 4
Channel Vw. Caravan Pk.
TA8: Brean 4A 26
Channing Cl. TA8: Bur S 2B 38
Chantry Cl. BS48: Nail 3C 6
Chantry Dr. BS22: Wor 3D 12
Chapel Barton BS48: Nail 2C 6
Chapel Cl. BS48: Nail 2E 7
Chapel Hill BS21: Clev 4D 4
BS40: Wrin 4B 16
Chapel La. BS49: C'ham 4F 9
BS49: C've 6H 9
Chapel St. TA8: Bur S 6A 36
Chard Cl. BS48: Nail 4F 7
Chard Rd. BS21: Clev 6D 4
Charlestone Rd. TA8: Bur S . . .5B 36
Charlock Cl. BS22: W Mare . . .2B 20
Charlock Rd. BS22: W Mare . . .2B 20
Charlotte Ct. TA9: High 4D 38
Charlton Av. BS23: W Mare . . .5D 18
Charlton Rd. BS23: W Mare . . .5D 18
Charnwood Dr. BS27: Ched . . .4G 35
Charterhouse Cl.
BS27: Ched 5H 35
BS48: Nail 3F 7
Charter Rd. BS22: W Mare 1H 19
Chaucer Rd. BS23: W Mare . . .5G 19
CHEDDAR 4G 35
Cheddar Bri. Pk.
BS27: Ched 5G 35
Cheddar Bus. Pk.
BS27: Ched 5F 35
Cheddar Cl. BS48: Nail 4F 7
TA8: Bur S 5C 36
Cheddarcoombe La.
BS25: S'ham, Star 2D 32
Cheddar Ct. BS27: Ched 4F 35
Cheddar Flds. BS27: Ched 4F 35
Cheddar Gorge Cheese
Company (Rural Village)
. . . . .3H 35
Cheddar Moor Drove
BS27: Ched 6G 35
Cheddar Rd. BS26: Axb 1C 34
Cheddar Sweet Kitchen 3H 35
Chelsfield BS48: Back 5G 7
Chelswood Av.
BS22: W Mare 1A 20
Chelswood Gdns.
BS22: W Mare 1B 20
CHELVEY 6D 6
Chelvey Ri. BS48: Nail 3G 7
Chelvey Rd.
BS48: Back, B'ley, Chelv, Nail
. . . . .6A 6 & 6C 6
Cherington Rd. BS48: Nail 3G 7
Cherry Av. BS21: Clev 5E 5
Cherry Cl. BS49: Yat 5B 8
Cherry Gdns. *BS22: Kew 3G 11*
(in Ardnave Holiday Pk.)
Cherry Gro. BS49: Yat 5B 8
Cherryhay BS21: Clev 6D 4
Cherry Rd. BS48: Nail 3D 6
Cherrywood Ri. BS22: Wor 5D 12
Cherrywood Rd. BS22: Wor . . .5D 12
Chescombe Rd. BS49: Yat 6B 8
Chesham Rd. Nth.
BS22: W Mare 1H 19
Chesham Rd. Sth.
BS22: W Mare 1H 19
Cheshire Av. BS24: Lock 4G 21
Chester Cl. BS24: W'ton V 1E 21
Chesterfield Cl. BS29: Ban 6B 22
Chesterton Dr. BS48: Nail 2G 7
Chestnut Av. BS22: Wor 6E 13
BS26: Axb 1B 34
Chestnut Chase BS48: Nail 1G 7

Chestnut Cl. BS29: Ban 6C 22
BS49: Cong 3D 14
Chestnut Dr. BS49: C'ham 4E 9
Chestnut Gro. BS21: Clev 3E 5
Chestnut La. BS24: B'don 4H 27
Chestnuts, The BS25: Wins . . .4A 32
BS27: Ched 3F 35
Chichester Cl. TA8: Bur S 5B 36
Chichester Way
BS24: W'ton V 1E 21
Chicken La. BS27: Ched 3F 35
Chimes, The BS48: Nail 4C 6
Chipping Cross BS21: Clev 6C 4
Chisholm Ter.
BS24: W Wick 1G 21
Christ Church Cl. BS48: Nail 2E 7
Christ Chu. Path Nth.
BS23: W Mare 1F 19
Christ Chu. Path Sth.
BS23: W Mare 1E 19
Christian Cl. BS22: Wor 4E 13
CHRISTON 4H 29
Christon Hill BS26: Chri 3G 29
Christon Rd.
BS26: Chri, Lox 5G 29
BS29: Ban 2B 30
Christon Ter. BS23: W Mare . . .1F 27
Church Cl. BS21: Clev 5A 4
BS49: Yat 6C 8
Church Ct. BS40: Redh 4H 17
Church Dr. BS49: Cong 3D 14
Church Hayes Cl. BS48: Nail 4E 7
Church Hayes Dr. BS48: Nail 4E 7
Church Ho. Rd. TA8: Berr 1A 36
CHURCHILL 5F 25
Churchill Av. BS21: Clev 5C 4
Churchill Bus. Pk.
BS23: W Mare 2G 19
Churchill Cl. BS21: Clev 5C 4
TA8: Bur S 2C 38
CHURCHILL GREEN 4C 24
Churchill Grn. BS25: C'hll 4B 24
Churchill Rd. BS23: W Mare . . .2G 19
Churchill Sports Cen. 4C 24
Churchlands Ct. TA8: Bur S . . .6A 36
Churchland Way
BS22: W Wick 1F 21
Church La. BS21: Tic 1B 6
BS24: Hut 1B 28
BS25: C'hll 4D 24
BS25: Wins 5G 31
BS26: Axb 1B 34
BS48: Back 6A 6
(not continuous)
BS48: Nail 3C 6
(not continuous)
BS49: Yat 6B 8
TA9: Bre K 3G 37
Church Rd. BS22: Wor 5B 12
BS25: Wins 5G 31
BS40: Redh 4H 17
BS49: Yat 6C 8
TA9: W Hunt 6B 38
Church St. BS27: Ched 4G 35
BS29: Ban 6D 22
TA9: High 4D 38
Church Vw. BS48: Wrax 2H 7
Church Wlk. BS40: Wrin 5B 16
Churchward Rd. BS22: Wor . . .4F 13
Claredge Ho. BS21: Clev 4D 4
Claremont Ct. BS21: Clev 3E 5
Claremont Cres.
BS23: W Mare 6B 10
Claremont Gdns. BS21: Clev 6E 5
BS48: Nail 3D 6
Clarence Gro. Rd.
BS23: W Mare 4E 19
Clarence Pl. BS23: W Mare . . .4D 18
Clarence Rd. E.
BS23: W Mare 4E 19
Clarence Rd. Nth.
BS23: W Mare 4D 18
Clarence Rd. Sth.
BS23: W Mare 4D 18
Clarendon Rd.
BS23: W Mare 1F 19
Clark Cl. BS48: Wrax 2G 7
Clarken Cl. BS48: Nail 3E 7
Clarkson Av. BS22: W Mare . . .6A 12
CLAVERHAM 4F 9
Claverham Cl. BS49: Yat 5D 8
Claverham Drove
BS49: C'ham 1B 8
Claverham Pk. BS49: C'ham 4F 9
Claverham Rd.
BS49: C'ham, Yat 6D 8
CLEEVE 5G 9
Cleeve Dr. BS49: C've 5G 9
Cleeve Hill Rd. BS40: Wrin . . .1B 16
BS49: C've 1B 16
Cleeve Pl. BS48: Nail 3G 7
CLEVEDON 4D 4
Clevedon Court 3G 5
Clevedon Hall Est.
BS21: Clev 4C 4
CLEVEDON HOSPITAL 4E 5
CLEVEDON HOSPITAL MINOR
INJURIES UNIT (MIU) 4E 5
Clevedon Miniature Railway . . .4B 4
Clevedon Pier 2C 4
Clevedon Rd. BS21: Tic 1E 7
BS23: W Mare 3D 18
BS48: Nail 1E 7
Clevedon School Sports Cen.
. . . . .2F 5
Clevedon Triangle Cen.
BS21: Clev 4D 4
Clevedon Wlk. BS48: Nail 2E 7
Cliff Rd. BS22: W Mare 4G 11
BS27: Ched 3H 35
Cliffs, The BS27: Ched 3H 35
Cliff St. BS27: Ched 4H 35
Clifton Av. BS23: W Mare 4E 19
Clifton Ct. BS21: Clev 5C 4
Clifton Rd. BS23: W Mare 3D 18
Cloisters Cft. TA8: Bur S 1B 38
Closemead BS21: Clev 6D 4
Clovelly Rd. BS22: Wor 5E 13
Clover Cl. BS21: Clev 4F 5
Clover Ct. BS22: W Mare 2B 20
Clover Rd. BS22: Wick L 1E 13
Clover Way TA9: High 3E 39
Clyce Rd. TA9: High 4C 38
Clynder Gro. BS21: Clev 1E 5
Coalbridge Cl. BS22: Wor 5D 12
Coates Gro. BS48: Nail 2G 7
Cobham Pde.
BS24: W Mare 4H 19
Cobley Cft. BS21: Clev 6C 4
Cobthorn Way BS49: Cong 2E 15
Cody Wlk. BS24: W Mare 5A 20
Coity Pl. BS21: Clev 3C 4
Coker Rd. BS22: Wor 5F 13
Coldharbour La.
BS23: W Mare 6D 18
Coleridge Ct. BS21: Clev 4D 4
Coleridge Gdns. TA8: Bur S . . .3B 36
Coleridge Rd. BS21: Clev 4C 4
BS23: W Mare 6F 19
Coleridge Va. Rd. E.
BS21: Clev 4D 4
Coleridge Va. Rd. Nth.
BS21: Clev 5C 4
Coleridge Va. Rd. Sth.
BS21: Clev 5C 4
Coleridge Va. Rd. W.
BS21: Clev 5C 4
College Ct. TA8: Bur S 6A 36
College St. TA8: Bur S 6A 36
Collett Cl. BS22: Wor 3G 13
Colliers Wlk. BS48: Nail 2E 7
Collingwood Cl. BS22: Wor . . .3C 12
Collum La. BS22: Kew 1B 12
Colombo Cres.
BS23: W Mare 6E 19
Colony, The TA8: Bur S 4A 36
Combeside BS48: Back 5G 7
Comer Rd. BS27: Ched 4F 35
Commerce Way TA9: High 5F 39
Commercial Way BS22: Wor . . .5F 13
Common La. BS25: C'hll 3B 24
Compton Dr. BS24: W'ton V . . .2C 20
Compton La. BS26: Axb 1A 34
Comrade Av. BS25: S'ham 3E 33
Concorde Dr. BS21: Clev 6B 4
Condor Cl. BS22: W Mare 1B 20
CONGRESBURY 3D 14
Conifer Way BS24: Lock 4C 20
Coniston Cres.
BS23: W Mare 5F 19
Connaught Pl.
BS23: W Mare 1D 18
Constable Dr. BS22: Wor 4D 12
Conway Cres. TA8: Bur S 4B 36
Conygar Cl. BS21: Clev 2F 5
Cooks Gdns. BS48: Wrax 2H 7
Cooks La. BS21: Clev 5G 5
BS29: Ban 5C 22
Cookson Cl. TA8: Bur S 2D 38
Coombe Rd. BS23: W Mare . . .1E 19
BS48: Nail 3D 6
Coombe Side TA9: Bre K 3H 37
Copley Gdns. BS22: Wor 5D 12
Copper Cl. BS27: Ched 3F 35
Copperfield Dr. BS22: Wor 3D 12
Coppice M. BS21: Clev 3C 4
Copse, The BS22: St Geo 5H 13
Copse Cl. BS24: W Mare 2G 27
Copse End BS25: Wins 1H 31
Copse Rd. BS21: Clev 3C 4
Coralberry Dr. BS22: Wor 6D 12
Corfe Cl. BS48: Nail 3D 6
Cormorant Cl. BS22: Wor 6D 12
Corner Cft. BS21: Clev 6D 4
Cornfields, The BS22: Wor 2D 12
Cornwallis Av. BS22: Wor 3C 12
Coronation Est.
BS23: W Mare 6F 19
Coronation Rd. BS22: Wor 5C 12
BS24: B'don 5A 28
BS29: Ban 6C 22
TA9: High 3D 38
Corondale Rd.
BS22: W Mare 1B 20
Corsham Dr. TA8: Bur S 5C 36
Corston BS24: W Mare 1G 27
Coryton BS22: Wor 5E 13
Cotman Wlk. BS22: Wor 5D 12
Cottage Row TA8: Bur S 1A 38
Cottages, The BS40: Wrin 5B 16
Coulson Dr. BS22: Wor 4F 13
Country Vw. Cvn. Pk.
BS22: Kew 2H 11
Court Av. BS49: Yat 6B 8
Court Cl. BS22: St Geo 5G 13
Court Dr. BS25: Sandf 5B 24
Courtenay Wlk. BS22: Wor 4E 13
Court Farm 4B 22
Court La. BS21: Clev 4G 5
BS25: S'ham 4F 33
Court Pl. BS22: Wor 5D 12
Court Rd. BS22: Kew 2G 11
Courtyard, The BS48: Nail 2E 7
Cowan Cl. TA8: Bur S 6C 36
COWSLIP GREEN 6F 17
Cowslip Grn. BS40: Redh 6F 17
Cox's Cave 3H 35
COX'S GREEN 6C 16
Cox's Grn. BS40: Wrin 6C 16
Coxway BS21: Clev 5E 5
Crabtree Pk. BS21: Clev 6C 4
Crabtree Path BS21: Clev 6C 4
Cranbourne Chase
BS23: W Mare 6G 11
Cranford Cl. BS22: W Mare 6B 12
Cranmore BS24: W Mare 1G 27
Cranwell Rd. BS24: Lock 4G 21
Crawford Cl. BS21: Clev 6B 4
Crediton BS22: Wor 5E 13
Crescent, The
BS22: W Mare 6H 11
(Milton Brow)
BS22: W Mare 5H 11
(Worlebury Hill Rd.)
BS24: Lym 6A 28
BS48: Back 6G 7
Cresswell Cl. BS22: Wor 5E 13
Creswick Way TA8: Bur S 5C 36
Crewkerne Cl. BS48: Nail 3H 7
Cribb's La. BS40: Redh 6H 17
Cricket Fld. Grn. BS48: Nail 2D 6
Cricklade Ct. BS48: Nail 3G 7
Croft, The BS21: Clev 3F 5
BS24: Hut 6C 20
BS27: Ched 3H 35
BS48: Back 5G 7
Cromer Rd. BS23: W Mare 4E 19
Cromwell Dr. BS22: Wor 3E 13
Crooked La. TA8: Bur S 4D 36
TA9: Bre K 3E 37
Crooke's La. BS22: Kew 3G 11
Crookwell Drove
BS49: Cong 6B 14
Crosby Hall BS23: W Mare 1D 18
Cross La. BS26: Axb, Cross . . .1A 34
Crossman Wlk. BS21: Clev 5F 5
Cross Moor Drove
BS26: Axb 3A 34
Crossmoor Rd. BS26: Axb 2A 34
Cross St. BS23: W Mare 2E 19
TA8: Bur S 6A 36
Crown Gdns. TA8: Bur S 6B 36
Crown Glass Pl. BS48: Nail 2E 7
Crown Ho. BS48: Nail 3C 6
Cubitt Cl. BS24: W Mare 5A 20
Cuck Hill BS25: S'ham 4E 33
Cufic La. BS27: Ched 2H 35
Cunningham Rd. TA8: Bur S . . .6C 36
Curlew Gdns. BS22: Wor 6D 12
Curzon Community Cinema, The
. . . . .4D 4
Cuthbert St. TA9: High 4D 38
Cygnet Cres. BS22: Wor 6D 12

D

Dag Hole BS27: Ched 3H 35
Dairy Cl. BS49: Yat 4A 8
Daley Cl. BS22: Wor 4F 13
Dalwood BS22: Wor 5E 13
Dame Ct. Cl. BS22: Wor 3D 12
Damson Rd. BS22: W Mare . . .1C 20
Daniel Cl. BS21: Clev 4F 5
Dark La. BS29: Ban 6E 23
BS48: Back . . . . . . .6B 6 & 6H 7
Darmead BS24: W'ton V 6F 13
Dartmouth Cl. BS22: Wor 5E 13
Dart Rd. BS21: Clev 6D 4
Daunton Cl. TA9: High 3D 38
Davis La. BS21: Clev 6D 4
Dawes Cl. BS21: Clev 6D 4
Deacons Cl. BS22: Wor 5C 12
Deacon Way TA8: Bur S 1B 38
Dean Cl. BS22: Wor 4F 13
Decoypool Drove
BS49: C'ham 1C 8
Deerleap BS25: S'ham 3F 33
Deer Mead BS21: Clev 6B 4
Delapre Rd. BS23: W Mare . . .6D 18
Dell, The BS22: Wor 3C 12
BS48: Nail 2D 6
Denning Ct. BS22: Wor 3F 13
Derham Cl. BS49: Yat 5B 8
Derham Ct. BS49: Yat 5B 8
Derham Pk. BS49: Yat 5B 8
Derwent Rd. BS23: W Mare . . .5G 19
De Salis Pk. BS24: W Wick . . .1H 21
Devonshire Ct.
BS23: W Mare 5E 19
Devonshire Rd.
BS23: W Mare 6E 19
Dewar Cl. TA8: Bur S 6C 36
Dial Hill Rd. BS21: Clev 2C 4
Diamond Batch
BS24: W'ton V 6F 13
Diamond Ct. BS24: Wor 6F 13
Diamond Farm Caravan
& Touring Pk.
TA8: Brean 6B 26
Diamond Mdw. TA8: Brean 6B 26
Dickenson Rd.
BS23: W Mare 3E 19
Dickensons Gro.
BS49: Cong 4E 15
Dinder Cl. BS48: Nail 3E 7
DINGHURST 5E 25
Dinghurst Rd. BS25: C'hll 5D 24
Disbrey M. BS24: Lock 4G 21
Doleberrow BS25: C'hll 6F 25
Dolebury Hill Fort 6F 25
Dolebury Warren Nature Reserve
. . . . .6F 25
Dolemoor La. BS49: Cong 3A 14
(Old Weston Rd.)
BS49: Cong 4A 14
(The Causeway)
Dolphin Sq. BS23: W Mare 2D 18
Donstan Rd. TA9: High 2D 38
Dorchester Cl. BS48: Nail 4D 6
Dormeads Vw.
BS24: W'ton V 2D 20
Dorset Cl. TA9: High 5E 39
Douglas Ct. BS23: W Mare 4F 19

E

F

G

Gordon Rd. BS23: W Mare 2F **19**
Gore Rd. TA8: Bur S 4A **36**
Gorge Walk 3H **35**
Goss Barton BS48: Nail 3D **6**
Goss Cl. BS48: Nail 3C **6**
Goss La. BS48: Nail 3C **6**
Goss Vw. BS48: Nail 3C **6**
Gough Pl. BS27: Ched 3F **35**
Gough's Cave 3H **35**
Grace Cl. BS49: Yat 5B **8**
Grace Rd. BS22: Wor 3F **13**
Gradwell Cl. BS22: Wor 4F **13**
Graham Rd. BS23: W Mare 2E **19**
Graitney Cl. BS49: C've 5G **9**
Grand Pier 2D **18**
Granfield Gdns. BS40: L'frd ...4G **25**
Grange Av. TA9: High 4E **39**
Grange Cl. BS23: Uph 2E **27**
Grange Farm Rd. BS49: Yat 4A **8**
Grange Rd. BS23: Uph 2E **27**
Grasmere Dr. BS23: W Mare 5F **19**
Grassmere Rd. BS49: Yat 5B **8**
Gt. Western Rd. BS21: Clev 4D **4**
Green, The BS24: Lock 5E **21**
  BS25: Wins 3H **31**
  BS48: Back 6A **6**
Greenacre BS22: W Mare 5H **11**
Greenacre Pl. Caravan Pk.
  TA9: Edith 1G **39**
Greenfield Cres. BS48: Nail 1E **7**
Greenfield Pl.
  BS23: W Mare 1C **18**
Greenfields Av. BS29: Ban 6C **22**
Greengage Cl.
  BS22: W Mare 1C **20**
Greenhayes BS27: Ched 3G **35**
Greenhill Cl. BS22: Wor 4E **13**
  BS48: Nail 2D **6**
Greenhill Cft. BS25: Sandf 5B **24**
Greenhill La. BS25: Sandf 5B **24**
Greenhill Rd. BS25: Sandf 5A **24**
Greenland Rd.
  BS22: W Mare 6B **12**
Green Pastures Rd.
  BS48: Wrax 1G **7**
Greenslade Gdns. BS48: Nail ...1D **6**
Greenway Pk. BS21: Clev 4F **5**
Greenwood Cl. TA9: W Hunt ...6C **38**
Greenwood Rd. BS22: Wor 5C **12**
Gregory Mead BS49: Yat 4A **8**
Greinton BS24: W Mare 1G **27**
Grenville Av. BS24: Lock 5E **21**
Grenville Rd. TA8: Bur S 6C **36**
Griffen Rd. BS24: W'ton V 2C **20**
Griffin Cl. BS22: Wor 5E **13**
Griffin Rd. BS21: Clev 4D **4**
Grove, The BS21: Clev 6B **4**
  BS25: Wins 2H **31**
  TA8: Bur S 4B **36**
Grove Dr. BS22: W Mare 6A **12**
Grove La. BS23: W Mare 1D **18**
Grove Mews, The
  TA8: Bur S 4B **36**
Grove Pk. Rd.
  BS23: W Mare 6D **10**
Grove Rd. BS22: W Mare 6A **12**
  BS23: W Mare 1D **18**
  BS29: Ban 5A **22**
  TA8: Bur S 5A **36**
Grove Sports Cen. 4D **6**
Gulliford Cl. TA9: High 3D **38**
Gulliford's Bank BS21: Clev 5E **5**
Gypsy La. BS27: Ched 5C **34**

H

Hafner Grn. BS24: W Mare 5A **20**
HALE COOMBE 5B **32**
Half Yd. BS40: L'frd 6B **16**
Hallam Rd. BS21: Clev 3C **4**
Hall Ter. TA8: Bur S 5A **36**
Halswell Rd. BS21: Clev 6D **4**
HAM 1E **37**
Hambledon Rd.
  BS22: St Geo 3G **13**
Hamilton Rd. BS23: W Mare ...6C **10**
Ham La. BS49: Yat 2A **8**
  TA8: Bur S 1B **38**
Hamlet, The BS48: Nail 1G **7**
Hampden Rd. BS22: Wor 5C **12**
Ham Rd. TA8: Berr 6B **26**
  TA9: Bre K 1D **36**
Hamwood Cl.
  BS24: W Mare 1H **27**
Hangstone Wlk. BS21: Clev 4C **4**
Hanham Way BS48: Nail 2B **6**
Hannah Dr. BS24: Lock 4G **21**
Hannah More Cl.
  BS27: Ched 4G **35**
  BS40: Wrin 5C **16**
Hannah More Ct.
  BS27: Ched 3G **35**
Hannah More Rd.
  BS48: Nail 3C **6**
Hannay Rd. BS27: Ched 2F **35**
Hanover Cl. BS22: Wor 3E **13**
Hansons Way BS21: Clev 5C **4**
Hans Price Cl.
  BS23: W Mare 1E **19**
Hans Price Sports Cen. 4F **19**
Hapil Cl. BS25: Sandf 5H **23**
Hapsburg Cl. BS22: Wor 3E **13**
Harbourne Cl. TA8: Bur S 5C **36**
Harp Rd. TA9: Bre K 5H **37**
Harptree BS24: W Mare 1G **27**
Harptree Cl. BS48: Nail 4D **6**
Harrier Path BS22: Wor 1C **20**
Hartland BS22: Wor 5E **13**
Harvest La. BS22: W Wick 1F **21**
Harvest Ri. BS26: Axb 2B **34**
Harvest Way BS22: Wor 2E **13**
Harvey Cl. BS22: Wor 3E **13**
Harwood Grn. BS22: Kew 4C **12**
Haslands BS48: Nail 4D **6**
Hatcher Cl. TA8: Bur S 2D **38**
Hatfield Rd. BS23: W Mare ...1G **19**
Havage Cl. TA9: High 2E **39**
Havage Drove BS24: E Rols ...1E **23**
Haversham Cl.
  BS22: W Mare 6B **12**
Havyatt Bus. Pk.
  BS40: Wrin 6C **16**
Havyatt Rd.
  BS40: L'frd, Wrin 6C **16**
Havyatt Trad. Est.
  BS40: Wrin 6C **16**
Hawke Rd. BS22: Kew 3C **12**
Hawkins Cl. TA8: Bur S 6C **36**
Hawksworth Dr. BS22: Wor ...3G **13**
Hawley Way TA8: Bur S 6C **36**
Hawthorn Coombe
  BS22: Wor 4B **12**
Hawthorn Cres. BS49: Yat 4A **8**
Hawthorn Gdns. BS22: Wor ...5B **12**
Hawthorn Hgts. BS22: Wor 4B **12**
Hawthorn Hill BS22: Wor 5B **12**
Hawthorn La. BS22: St Geo ...5G **13**
Hawthorn Pk. BS22: Wor 4C **12**
Hawthorns, The BS21: Clev 4C **4**
Hawthorn Way BS48: Nail 2F **7**
Hayes, The BS27: Ched 4G **35**
Hayward Av. BS24: W Wick 1F **21**
Hayward Cl. BS21: Clev 6C **4**
Haywood Cl. BS24: W Mare ...2G **27**
Haywood Gdns.
  BS24: W Mare 2G **27**
Hazelbury Cl. BS48: Nail 2E **7**
Hazelbury Rd. BS48: Nail 3D **6**
Hazeldene Rd.
  BS23: W Mare 1G **19**
Hazell Cl. BS21: Clev 6E **5**
Heal Cl. TA8: Bur S 2D **38**
Heathfield Rd. BS48: Nail 2E **7**
Heathfield Way BS48: Nail 2E **7**
Heathgate BS49: Yat 5B **8**
Heath Gates *BS48: Nail 2F 7*
  (off Heath Rd.)
Heathgates BS23: W Mare 5D **18**
Heath Rd. BS48: Nail 1F **7**
  (not continuous)
Hector Cl. BS24: Lock 5H **21**
Hedge Cl. BS22: W Wick 6F **13**
Hedges, The BS22: St Geo 5G **13**
Hedges Cl. BS21: Clev 6B **4**
Helens Rd. BS25: Sandf 5B **24**
Helicopter Mus., The 4C **20**
Heligan Wlk.
  BS24: W'ton V 2C **20**
Hellier's La. BS27: Ched 5C **34**
Helston Rd. BS48: Nail 3G **7**
Hemming Way BS24: Hut 6C **20**
Hendon Cl. TA9: High 2E **39**
Henley La. BS49: Yat 6D **8**
Henley Lodge BS49: Yat 6D **8**
Henley Pk. BS49: Yat 6C **8**
Henry Butt Ho.
  BS23: W Mare 1E 19
  (off Boulevard)
Herbert Rd. BS21: Clev 3D **4**
  TA8: Bur S 5A **36**
Herluin Way BS22: W Mare ...2B **20**
  BS23: W Mare 3G **19**
Heron Cl. BS22: W Mare 6C **12**
Hestercombe Cl.
  BS24: W'ton V 2C **20**
Hidcote M. BS24: W'ton V 2C **20**
HIGHBRIDGE 4E **39**
Highbridge & Burnham Station (Rail)
  ....4E **39**
Highbridge Quay TA9: High ...4D **38**
Highbridge Rd. TA8: Bur S 1B **38**
Highburn Cl. TA8: Bur S 3C **38**
Highbury Pde.
  BS23: W Mare 6C **10**
Highbury Rd. BS23: W Mare ...6C **10**
Highdale Av. BS21: Clev 4D **4**
Highdale Rd. BS21: Clev 4D **4**
Highfield Rd.
  BS24: W Mare 2G **27**
Highgrove Wlk.
  BS24: W'ton V 1E **21**
Highland Cl. BS22: W Mare ...5H **11**
Highlands La.
  BS24: W'ton V 1E **21**
High St. BS22: Wor 6C **12**
  BS23: W Mare 1D **18**
  (not continuous)
  BS26: Axb 1A **34**
  BS29: Ban 1A **30**
  BS40: Wrin 4B **16**
  BS48: Nail 2E **7**
  BS49: C'ham 4F **9**
  BS49: Cong 3D **14**
  BS49: Yat 4B **8**
  TA8: Bur S 1A **38**
Hilcot Gro. BS22: W Mare 6H **11**
Hildesheim Bri.
  BS23: W Mare 2E **19**
Hildesheim Cl.
  BS23: W Mare 2F **19**
Hildesheim Ct.
  BS23: W Mare 2E 19
  (off Station Rd.)
Hillcote BS24: W Mare 3H **27**
Hillcote Mans.
  BS23: W Mare 6C **10**
Hill Crest BS49: Cong 2E **15**
Hillcrest Cl. BS48: Nail 3E **7**
Hillcrest Rd. BS48: Nail 3E **7**
Hillcroft Cl. BS22: W Mare 5G **11**
Hilldale Rd. BS48: Back 6B **6**
HILLEND 1H **29**
Hill End BS22: Wor 4C **12**
HILLFIELD 4F **35**
Hillfield BS27: Ched 4G **35**
Hillfield Path BS27: Ched 3F **35**
Hillgrove Ter. BS23: Uph 2D **26**
Hillier's La. BS25: C'hll 5D **24**
Hill La. BS25: Row 2G **33**
  TA9: Bre K, E Brnt 3G **37**
Hill Lea Gdns. BS27: Ched 3G **35**
Hillmead BS40: L'frd 4G **25**
Hillmer Ri. BS29: Ban 6B **22**
Hill Moor BS21: Clev 5E **5**
Hill Pk. BS49: Cong 2E **15**
Hill Path BS29: Ban 1D **30**
Hill Rd. BS21: Clev 3C **4**
  BS22: Wor 5C **12**
  BS23: W Mare 1F **19**
  BS25: Sandf 6H **23**
Hill Rd. E. BS22: Wor 5C **12**
Hillsborough Gdns.
  TA8: Bur S 4B **36**
Hillsborough Ho.
  BS23: W Mare 5G **19**
HILLSIDE 1B **34**
Hillside BS26: Axb 1B **34**
Hillside Gdns.
  BS22: W Mare 6H **11**
Hillside Rd. BS21: Clev 4D **4**
  BS24: B'don 3H **27**
  BS48: Back 6A **6**
Hillside W. BS24: Hut 6D **20**
Hillview Av. BS21: Clev 5D **4**
Hill Vw. Ct. BS22: W Mare 1B **20**
Hillview Pk. Homes
  BS22: W Mare 1B **20**
Hill Vw. Rd. BS23: W Mare ...2G **19**
Hillyfields BS25: Wins 3B **32**
Hillyfields Way BS25: Wins ...3A **32**
Hinckley Cl. BS22: St Geo 4G **13**
Hind Pitts BS25: S'ham 4E **33**
Hinton BS24: W Mare 1G **27**
Hippisley Dr. BS26: Axb 1C **34**
Hither Grn. BS21: Clev 5F **5**
Hither Grn. Ind. Est.
  BS21: Clev 5F **5**
Hobart Rd. BS23: W Mare 6F **19**
Hobbiton Rd. BS22: Wor 2E **13**
Hobbs Ct. BS48: Nail 2F **7**
Hogarth M. BS22: Wor 4E **13**
Hogarth Wlk. BS22: Wor 4E **13**
Holford Cl. BS48: Nail 3E **7**
Holland Rd. BS21: Clev 6B **4**
Holland St. BS23: W Mare 1G **19**
Holloway La.
  BS25: Row, S'ham 3G **33**
Hollow La. BS22: Wor 4D **12**
Hollowmead BS49: C'ham 5E **9**
Hollowmead Cl.
  BS49: C'ham 5F **9**
Hollow Rd. BS25: S'ham 3E **33**
Holly Cl. BS22: Wor 6E **13**
  BS48: Nail 1G **7**
Holly La. BS21: Clev 1F **5**
Hollyman Wlk. BS21: Clev 4F **5**
Holly Ri. *BS22: Kew 3G 11*
  (in Ardnave Holiday Pk.)
Holm Cl. TA8: Bur S 2B **38**
Holm Rd. BS24: Hut 1C **28**
Holms Rd. BS23: W Mare 4G **19**
Holts Ho. TA8: Bur S 2B **38**
Holts Way BS23: W Mare 4F **19**
Holwell La. BS27: Ched 3E **35**
Home Cl. BS40: Wrin 4C **16**
Home Farm Ct.
  BS22: St Geo 4G 13
  (off Brimbleworth La.)
Home Farm Holiday Pk.
& Country Pk.
  TA9: Edith 6E **37**
Homefield BS24: Lock 4D **20**
  BS49: Cong 4E **15**
Homefield Cl. BS24: Lock 4E **21**
  BS25: Wins 2H **31**
Homefield Ind. Est.
  BS24: Lock 4E **21**
Homeground BS21: Clev 5E **5**
Homelane Ho. TA8: Bur S 5B **36**
Homestead, The BS21: Clev 4C **4**
Homestead Way
  BS25: Wins 3A **32**
HONEY HALL 2C **24**
Honeyhall La. BS49: Cong 2C **24**
Honeysuckle Pl.
  BS24: W'ton V 1E **21**
Honiton BS22: Wor 5E **13**
Honiton Rd. BS21: Clev 6E **5**
Hooper Cl. TA8: Bur S 2D **38**
  TA9: High 3F **39**
Hopkins St. BS23: W Mare 1E **19**
Hopwoods Cnr. BS27: Ched ...3G **35**
Horn's La. BS26: Axb 1A **34**
HORSECASTLE 4A **8**
Horsecastle Cl. BS49: Yat 4A **8**
Horsecastle Farm Rd.
  BS49: Yat 4A **8**
Horseleaze La. BS25: Star 2D **32**
Horwood Rd. BS48: Nail 3F **7**
Hosegood Dr.
  BS24: W Mare 5A **20**
Houlgate Way BS26: Axb 1A **34**
Howard Cl. TA8: Bur S 6C **36**
Howitt Way BS24: W'ton V 2D **20**
Hudson St. TA8: Bur S 1B **38**
Hughenden Rd.
  BS23: W Mare 1G **19**
Huish Cl. TA9: High 3D **38**
Huntley Gro. BS48: Nail 3G **7**
Hunt's La. BS49: C'ham 5E **9**
Huntsmans Ridge
  BS27: Ched 4H **35**
HUNTSPILL 6C **38**

Lwr. Norton La.—Newton Rd.

Lwr. Norton La. BS22: Kew ...3H **11**
(Kewside)
BS22: Kew ...3C **12**
(Queen's Way)
Lwr. Parade Ground Rd.
BS24: Lock ...4F **21**
Lwr. Queen's Rd. BS21: Clev ...4D **4**
LOXTON ...6G 29
Loxton Rd. BS23: W Mare ...6F **19**
Lundy Dr. TA8: Bur S ...2B **38**
Lunty Mead BS48: Back ...6F **7**
Lychgate Pk. BS24: Lock ...5E **21**
Lyddon Rd. BS22: Wor ...4F **13**
Lyde La. BS27: Ched ...6H **35**
LYE CROSS ...6G 17
Lye Cross Rd. BS40: Redh ...6G **17**
Lyefield Rd.
BS22: Kew, Wor ...3C **12**
LYE HOLE ...5H 17
Lye Hole La. BS40: Redh ...5H **17**
Lyes, The BS49: Cong ...4D **14**
Lynch, The BS25: Wins ...4H **31**
Lynch Cl. BS22: Wor ...4D **12**
Lynch Cres. BS25: Wins ...4H **31**
Lynch La. BS27: Ched ...3H **35**
Lynchmead BS25: Wins ...4H **31**
Lyncombe Dr. BS25: Sandf ...5C **24**
Lyncombe La.
BS25: C'hll, Sandf ...1D **32**
Lyndhurst Rd.
BS23: W Mare ...5E **19**
Lynmouth Cl. BS22: Wor ...5E **13**
Lynton Rd. TA8: Bur S ...1B **38**
Lynx Cres. BS24: W Mare ...6H **19**
Lyons Ct. BS23: W Mare ...2F **19**
Lypstone Cl. BS24: W'ton V ...1E **21**
Lypstone Farm
BS24: W'ton V ...1E **21**

M

McCrae Rd. BS24: Lock ...4F **21**
Macfarlane Chase
BS23: W Mare ...4G **19**
Macleod Cl. BS21: Clev ...5A **4**
Macquarie Farm Cl.
BS49: Yat ...4A **8**
Madam La. BS22: Wor ...5D **12**
(Orchard Cl.)
BS22: Wor ...4E **13**
(Wynter Cl.)
Madden Cl. TA8: Bur S ...6C **36**
Maddocks Slade TA8: Bur S ...5A **36**
Madeira Ct. BS23: W Mare ...1C **18**
Madeira Rd. BS21: Clev ...4D **4**
BS23: W Mare ...6C **10**
Magdalen Way BS22: Wor ...4E **13**
Magellan Cl. BS22: Wor ...3D **12**
Magistrates' Court
North Somerset ...5G 13
Magnolia Av. BS22: Wor ...6E **13**
Magnolia Cl. BS22: W Mare ...2C **20**
Magnolia Grange
BS22: Wor ...5D **12**
Magnolia M. *BS22: Kew ...3G **11***
(in Ardnave Holiday Pk.)
Magpie Cl. BS22: Wor ...1C **20**
TA8: Bur S ...4B **36**
Maidstone Gro.
BS24: W Mare ...2G **27**
MAINES BATCH ...4B 16
Main Rd. BS24: Hut ...1B **28**
BS48: Back, B'ley ...6A **6**
BS49: C've ...6G **9**
TA9: W Hunt ...6C **38**
Mallard Pl. TA9: High ...3C **38**
Mallard Wlk. BS22: W Mare ...1C **20**
Mallow Cl. BS21: Clev ...5E **5**
Maltings, The BS22: Wor ...5D **12**
Maltlands BS22: W Mare ...2B **20**
Malvern Rd. BS23: W Mare ...4E **19**
Manilla Cres. B
S23: W Mare ...6C **10**
Manilla Pl. BS23: W Mare ...6C **10**
Manmoor La. BS21: Clev ...6G **5**
Manor Ct. BS23: W Mare ...1G **19**
BS24: Lock ...5E **21**
BS48: Back ...6A **6**
Mnr. Farm Cvn. Pk.
BS23: Uph ...2E **27**
Mnr. Farm Cl.
BS24: W Mare ...1H **27**
Mnr. Farm Cres.
BS24: W Mare ...1H **27**
Manor Gdns. BS22: Kew ...3H **11**
BS24: Lock ...5E **21**
Manor Grange BS24: B'don ...4H **27**
Manor Ride TA9: Bre K ...3H **37**
Manor Rd. BS23: W Mare ...6F **11**
TA8: Bur S ...6B **36**
Manor Valley
BS23: W Mare ...6G **11**
Mansfield Av.
BS23: W Mare ...1H **19**
Mansfield Cl.
BS23: W Mare ...1H **19**
Mantle Cl. BS21: Clev ...5E **5**
Maple Cl. BS23: W Mare ...1G **19**
Maple Ct. BS23: W Mare ...6C **10**
Maple Dr. TA8: Bur S ...1B **38**
Maples, The BS48: Nail ...3C **6**
Mapleton La. BS25: Star ...1D **32**
Maple Vw. *BS22: Kew ...3G **11***
(in Ardnave Holiday Pk.)
Marchfields Way
BS23: W Mare ...3F **19**
Marconi Cl. BS23: W Mare ...2H **19**
Marconi Dr. TA9: High ...2D **38**
Margaret Cres. TA8: Bur S ...2A **38**
Marindin Dr. BS22: Wor ...3F **13**
Marine Dr. TA8: Bur S ...1B **38**
Marine Hill BS21: Clev ...2C **4**
Marine Pde. BS21: Clev ...3C **4**
BS23: W Mare ...4D **18**
(Beach Rd.)
BS23: W Mare ...6B **10**
(Claremont Cres.)
Mariners Cl. BS22: W Mare ...6B **12**
BS48: Back ...6G **7**
Mariners Dr. BS48: Back ...6G **7**
Maritime Wlk. TA9: High ...2D **38**
Market Av. BS22: St Geo ...4G **13**
Market Ind. Est. BS49: Yat ...4B **8**
Market La. BS23: W Mare ...1D **18**
Market St. TA9: High ...4E **39**
Market Ter. TA9: High ...4E **39**
Mark Rd. TA9: High, W'fld ...4F **39**
Marlborough Ct. TA8: Bur S ...4B **36**
Marlborough Dr. BS22: Wor ...5E **13**
Marle Pits BS48: Back ...6F **7**
Marlowe Ho. BS23: W Mare ...5F **19**
Marron Cl. BS26: Axb ...1B **34**
Marsh Rd. BS49: Yat ...6B **8**
Marson Rd. BS21: Clev ...4D **4**
Martindale Ct.
BS22: W Mare ...1B **20**
Martindale Rd.
BS22: W Mare ...1B **20**
Martin's Cl. TA8: Bur S ...2A **36**
Martins Gro. BS22: Wor ...5C **12**
Martock BS24: W Mare ...1F **27**
Marwood Cl. TA8: Bur S ...5C **36**
Mason's Way BS27: Ched ...4H **35**
Maunsell Rd.
BS24: W'ton V ...2C **20**
Max Mill La.
BS25: Ban, Wins ...2D **30**
Maxwell Dr. TA9: High ...2D **38**
Mayfair Av. BS48: Nail ...3E **7**
Mayfield Av. BS22: Wor ...6C **12**
Mayflower Ct. TA9: High ...3E **39**
Mayflower Gdns. BS48: Nail ...2G **7**
Maynard Cl. BS21: Clev ...4F **5**
Maysmead La. BS40: L'frd ...3H **25**
May Tree Cl. BS48: Nail ...3C **6**
Mead, The BS25: S'ham ...3E **33**
Mead Cl. BS27: Ched ...5G **35**
Mead La. BS24: Nye, Sandf ...4F **23**
BS25: Sandf ...5G **23**
Meadowbank BS22: Wor ...4D **12**
Meadow Cl. BS48: Back ...6H **7**
BS48: Nail ...1E **7**
TA9: High ...3D **38**
Meadow Cft. BS24: W Mare ...1H **27**
Meadowcroft Dr. TA8: Bur S ...5C **36**
Meadow Dr. BS24: Lock ...5F **21**
Meadowland BS49: Yat ...4A **8**
Meadowlands BS22: St Geo ...5G **13**
Meadow Pl. BS22: St Geo ...4H **13**
Meadow Rd. BS21: Clev ...4E **5**
Meadows End BS25: C'hll ...5D **24**
Meadow St. BS23: W Mare ...2E **19**
BS26: Axb ...2B **34**
Meadow Vw. TA9: High ...5C **38**
Meadow Vs. *BS23: W Mare ...1E **19***
(off Prospect Pl.)
Mead Va.
BS22: W Mare, Wor ...6C **12**
Meadway Av. BS48: Nail ...2D **6**
Mearcombe La.
BS24: B'don ...6D **28**
Meare BS24: W Mare ...1F **27**
Meer Wall BS24: Cong ...1H **23**
BS25: Cong ...1H **23**
Meeting Ho. La.
BS49: C'ham, C've ...3G **9**
Melbourne Ter. BS21: Clev ...5D **4**
Memorial Rd. BS40: Wrin ...5C **16**
Mendip Av. BS22: Wor ...5C **12**
Mendip Cl. BS26: Axb ...1B **34**
BS48: Nail ...3E **7**
BS49: Yat ...6B **8**
Mendip Edge BS24: W Mare ...3F **27**
Mendip Gdns. BS49: Yat ...6B **8**
Mendip Model Motor Racing Circuit
...5F 27
Mendip Ri. BS24: Lock ...5F **21**
Mendip Rd. BS23: W Mare ...2G **19**
BS24: Lock ...5G **21**
BS49: Yat ...5A **8**
Mendip Va. Trad. Est.
BS27: Ched ...4F **35**
Mendip Way TA8: Bur S ...6B **36**
Merlin Cl. BS22: Wor ...1C **20**
Merryfield Rd. BS24: Lock ...3F **21**
Merton Dr. BS24: W'ton V ...1E **21**
Methwyn Cl. BS22: W Mare ...2A **20**
Mewswell Dr. BS27: Ched ...2F **35**
MIDDLE BURNHAM ...5D 36
Middle Fld. La.
TA9: W Hunt ...6A **38**
Middle Moor La.
BS27: Ched ...4C **34**
Middle St. TA9: Bre K ...1E **37**
Middle Yeo Grn. BS48: Nail ...1D **6**
Midford BS24: W Mare ...1F **27**
Midhaven Ri. BS22: Wor ...3C **12**
Milburn Rd. BS23: W Mare ...2F **19**
Milbury Gdns.
BS22: W Mare ...5H **11**
Milestone Ct. BS22: St Geo ...5H **13**
Millbourne Rd. BS27: Ched ...4H **35**
Millcross BS21: Clev ...6C **4**
Millennium M. BS49: Cong ...3E **15**
Miller Cl. BS23: W Mare ...1F **19**
Miller's Ri. BS22: Wor ...3E **13**
Millier Rd. BS49: C've ...5G **9**
Mill La. BS40: Wrin ...6C **16**
BS49: Cong ...3D **14**
Mill Leg BS49: Cong ...3D **14**
Millstone Cl. BS24: W'ton V ...1D **20**
Mill Stream Cl. BS26: Axb ...2A **34**
MILTON ...6A 12
Milton Av. BS23: W Mare ...1G **19**
Milton Brow BS22: W Mare ...6H **11**
Milton Cl. BS48: Nail ...1E **7**
Milton Grn. BS22: W Mare ...6A **12**
MILTON HILL ...4H 11
Milton Hill BS22: W Mare ...5H **11**
Milton Pk. Rd.
BS22: W Mare ...6A **12**
Milton Ri. BS22: W Mare ...6H **11**
Milton Rd. BS22: W Mare ...1F **19**
BS23: W Mare ...1F **19**
Milverton BS24: W Mare ...1F **27**
Mizzymead Cl. BS48: Nail ...3D **6**
Mizzymead Recreation Cen. ...3E 7
Mizzymead Ri. BS48: Nail ...3D **6**
Mizzymead Rd. BS48: Nail ...3E **7**
Monks Hill
BS22: Kew, W Mare ...4H **11**
Monks Way TA8: Bur S ...1B **38**
Monkton Av. BS24: W Mare ...1G **27**
Montacute Cir.
BS24: W'ton V ...1D **20**
Montpelier BS23: W Mare ...6F **11**
Montpelier E. BS23: W Mare ...6F **11**
Montpelier Path
BS23: W Mare ...1E **19**
Moorcroft Rd. BS24: Hut ...6C **20**
Moor Drove BS49: Cong ...6C **14**
Moor End Spout BS48: Nail ...1D **6**
Moorfield Rd. BS48: Back ...5F **7**
Moorfields Ct. BS48: Nail ...2D **6**
Moorfields Ho. BS48: Nail ...2C **6**
Moorfields Rd. BS48: Nail ...2D **6**
Moor Grn. BS26: Axb ...2B **34**
Moorham Rd. BS25: Wins ...2A **32**
Moorland Rd.
BS23: W Mare ...5D **18**
Moorlands Cl. BS48: Nail ...2D **6**
Moorland St. BS26: Axb ...2B **34**
Moor La. BS21: Clev ...5E **5**
(Beaconsfield Rd.)
BS21: Clev ...5F **5**
(Cook's La.)
BS21: Tic ...1A **6**
BS21: Walt G ...1H **5**
BS22: Wor ...6D **12**
BS24: Hut ...5B **20**
BS24: W'ton V ...2C **20**
BS48: Back ...6F **7**
Moor Pk. BS21: Clev ...5E **5**
(not continuous)
Moor Rd. BS29: Ban ...1B **22**
BS49: Yat ...2B **8**
Moorside BS49: Yat ...4B **8**
Moorside Ct. BS21: Clev ...5E **5**
Morgan Cl. BS22: W Wick ...1F **21**
Morgans Hill Cl. BS48: Nail ...4D **6**
Morland Rd. TA9: High ...3D **38**
Morlands Ind. Pk.
TA9: High ...3D **38**
Morston Ct. BS22: W Mare ...2A **20**
Moseley Gro. BS23: Uph ...1E **27**
Mountbatten Cl. BS22: Kew ...3C **12**
TA8: Bur S ...4A **36**
Mud La. BS49: C'ham ...3D **8**
Mulberry Cl. BS22: Wor ...6D **12**
BS48: Back ...6G **7**
Mulberry La. BS24: B'don ...5A **28**
Mulberry Rd. BS49: Cong ...4E **15**
Mulholland Way TA9: High ...2D **38**
Munscroft Ct. BS23: W Mare ...1F **19**
Myrtleberry Mead
BS22: Wick L ...2E **13**
Myrtle Dr. TA8: Bur S ...6A **36**
Myrtle Gdns. BS49: Yat ...5C **8**
Myrtles, The BS24: Hut ...1B **28**
Myrtle Tree Cres.
BS22: Kew ...1G **11**

N

NAILSEA ...2E 7
Nailsea & Backwell Station (Rail)
...5F 7
Nailsea Moor La. BS48: Nail ...5A **6**
Nailsea Pk. BS48: Nail ...2F **7**
Nailsea Pk. Cl. BS48: Nail ...1F **7**
Naish Rd. TA8: Bur S ...2A **36**
Nates La. BS40: Wrin ...6D **16**
Naunton Way
BS22: W Mare ...5H **11**
Nelson Ct. BS22: Wor ...3C **12**
Netherton Wood La.
BS48: Nail ...6C **6**
Netherways BS21: Clev ...6B **4**
Neva Rd. BS23: W Mare ...3E **19**
Newbourne Rd.
BS22: W Mare ...2A **20**
Newbridge Drove
TA9: E Hunt ...6F **39**
Newbridge La. TA9: E Hunt ...6F **39**
(not continuous)
New Bristol Rd. BS22: Wor ...6C **12**
New Church Rd. BS23: Uph ...1D **26**
Newcombe La. BS25: Wins ...4B **32**
Newland Rd.
BS23: W Mare ...3F **19**
Newlands Grn. BS21: Clev ...6E **5**
Newmans La. TA9: E Hunt ...6H **39**
Newport Cl. BS21: Clev ...5C **4**
New Rd. BS21: Clev ...5D **4**
BS25: C'hll ...6F **25**
BS25: Row, S'ham ...3E **33**
BS29: Ban ...5A **22**
TA9: E Hunt, W Hunt ...6C **38**
NEWTON ...3D 38
Newton Cl. TA8: Bur S ...3A **36**
Newton Grn. BS48: Nail ...4C **6**
Newton Rd. BS23: W Mare ...4E **19**

A-Z Weston-Super-Mare 47

Purn Way BS24: B'don 4G **27**
Puttingthorpe Dr.
BS22: W Mare 2A **20**
Puxton La.
BS24: E Rols, Hew, Pux
.... 1G **23**
Puxton Rd.
BS24: E Rols, Pux 1D **22**
Pylewell La. BS25: Star 1D **32**
Pyne Point BS21: Clev 4C **4**

Q

Quantock Cl. TA8: Bur S 6B **36**
Quantock Ct. TA8: Bur S 2A **38**
Quantock Rd.
BS23: W Mare 5D **18**
Quarry Ri. BS24: W Mare 3F **27**
Quarry Rd. BS25: Sandf 1A **32**
Quarry Way BS48: Nail 2D **6**
Queens Rd. BS21: Clev 4D **4**
BS23: W Mare 6D **10**
BS29: Ban 6C **22**
BS48: Nail 3C **6**
Queens Sq. *BS21: Clev 4D 4*
(off Station Rd.)
TA9: High 3C **38**
Queen's Way
BS22: Kew, St Geo, Wor .. 3C **12**
Queensway Cen. BS22: Wor ... 5F **13**

R

Racurium Lodge BS26: Axb ... 1A **34**
Raglan Pl. BS23: W Mare 1C **18**
Railway Wlk. BS25: Wins 2H **31**
Rainham Ct. BS23: W Mare ... 6C **10**
Raleigh Gdns. TA8: Bur S 6C **36**
Ramsay Cl. BS22: Wor 3C **12**
Ramsay Way TA8: Bur S 6C **36**
Ranscombe Av. BS22: Wor 5B **12**
Ransford BS21: Clev 6B **4**
Rapide Way BS24: W Mare ... 5H **19**
Rattigan Cl. TA8: Bur S 1C **38**
Raven Cl. BS22: W Mare 6C **12**
Ravensworth Ter.
TA8: Bur S 6B **36**
Rawlins Av. BS22: Wor 2E **13**
Rayneswood BS23: W Mare ... 1F **19**
Reads Gdn. *BS26: Axb 1A 34*
(off Old Church Rd.)
Rectors Way BS23: W Mare ... 3F **19**
Rectory Cl. BS48: Wrax 2G **7**
Rectory Dr. BS49: Yat 6C **8**
TA8: Bur S 5B **36**
Rectory La. BS24: B'don 5A **28**
Rectory Lawn TA8: Bur S 5B **36**
Rectory Pl. TA8: Bur S 5C **36**
Rectory Rd. TA8: Bur S 5B **36**
Rectory Way BS49: Yat 6C **8**
Redacre BS40: Redh 4H **17**
Redcliffe St. BS27: Ched 4H **35**
Redcroft BS40: Redh 4H **17**
REDHILL 4H **17**
Red Hill BS40: Redh 6G **17**
Red Lodge Bus. Pk.
BS24: W Wick 5H **13**
Redshard La. BS40: L'frd 2H **25**
Redwing Dr. BS22: Wor 6D **12**
Redwood Cl. BS48: Nail 2G **7**
Reed Way BS22: St Geo 4G **13**
Regal Ct. TA9: High 4D **38**
Regency Cl. TA8: Bur S 3A **36**
Regent St. BS23: W Mare 2D **18**
TA8: Bur S 6A **36**
Rendcomb Cl.
BS22: W Mare 5H **11**
Retreat Caravan Park, The
TA8: Bur S 3A **36**
Rhodyate, The BS29: Ban 1E **31**
Rhodyate Hill
BS49: C've, Cong 2E **15**
Rhodyate La. BS49: C've 6F **9**
Rhyne Ter. BS23: Uph 1D **26**
Rhyne Vw. BS48: Nail 3B **6**
Richards Cl. BS22: Wor 3F **13**
Richmond Grn. BS48: Nail 3F **7**
Richmond St.
BS23: W Mare 2D **18**
Ricketts La. BS22: Wor 5E **13**
Rickford Rd. BS48: Nail 3F **7**
Rickyard Rd. BS40: Wrin 5C **16**
Ridge, The BS49: Yat 5B **8**
Ridgeway BS48: Nail 3C **6**
Ridgeway, The
BS22: W Mare 5H **11**
Ridgeway Av.
BS23: W Mare 3E **19**
Ringwood Gro.
BS23: W Mare 6G **11**
Rippleside Rd. BS21: Clev 2E **5**
Risedale Rd. BS25: Wins 3A **32**
Ritz Cinema, The
Burnham-on-Sea 6A **36**
Rivendell BS22: Wor 3E **13**
Riverbed Ho. TA9: High 4D **38**
River Mead BS21: Clev 6D **4**
River Path BS21: Clev 4D **4**
(Arundel Rd.)
BS21: Clev 6E **5**
(Claremont Gdns.)
BS21: Clev 6D **4**
(River Mead)
Riverside BS29: Ban 3D **22**
Riverside Cl. BS21: Clev 5B **4**
BS22: St Geo 4G **13**
River Wlk. BS22: St Geo 5H **13**
Riverway BS48: Nail 1F **7**
Robert Nightingale Ct.
BS23: W Mare 3F **19**
Robin Cl. BS22: W Mare 1C **20**
Robin Dr. BS24: Hut 1C **28**
Robin La. BS21: Clev 2D **4**
Robinson Cl. BS48: Back 6A **6**
Robinson Way BS48: Back 6A **6**
Rob-Lynne Ct. BS25: Wins 3H **31**
Rochester Cl.
BS24: W Mare 2G **27**
Rock Av. BS48: Nail 2C **6**
Rockeries Dr. BS25: Wins 3H **31**
Rockfield Cotts.
BS22: W Mare 6H **11**
Rockingham Gro.
BS23: W Mare 6G **11**
Rock Rd. BS49: Yat 6C **8**
Rocky La. BS29: Ban 1D **30**
Rodney BS24: W Mare 1G **27**
Rodney Rd. BS48: Back 6G **7**
Roebuck Cl. BS22: Wor 3E **13**
Roman Rd.
BS24: W Mare, B'don 3G **27**
BS25: Sandf 5H **23**
Rookery Cl. BS22: Wor 4C **12**
Roper's La. BS40: Wrin 4B **16**
Rope Wlk. BS48: Back 6A **6**
Rosedale Av. BS23: W Mare ... 2G **19**
Rose Gdns. BS22: Wor 3F **13**
Roseneath Av. TA8: Berr 1A **36**
Rosetree Paddock TA8: Berr ... 1A **36**
Rosewood Av. TA8: Bur S 1C **38**
Rosewood Cl. TA8: Bur S 6B **36**
Rosewood Dr. TA8: Bur S 1C **38**
Roslyn Av. BS22: W Mare 6A **12**
Rossendale Cl. BS22: Wor 4D **12**
Round Oak Gro. BS27: Ched ... 3F **35**
Round Oak Rd. BS27: Ched ... 3F **35**
Rowan Cl. BS48: Nail 2G **7**
Rowan Ct. *BS22: Kew 3G 11*
(in Ardnave Holiday Pk.)
Rowan Pl. BS24: W'ton V 6F **13**
Rowan Way BS40: L'frd 4G **25**
ROWBERROW 2G **33**
ROWBERROW BOTTOM 3H **33**
Rowberrow La.
BS25: Row, S'ham 1F **33**
Rowberrow Way BS48: Nail 3E **7**
Rows, The BS22: Wor 5C **12**
Royal Ct. *BS23: W Mare 5D 18*
(off Royal Sands)
Royal Cres. BS23: W Mare 1D **18**
Royal Pde. BS23: W Mare 1D **18**
Royal Sands BS23: W Mare ... 5D **18**
(not continuous)
Roynon Way BS27: Ched 4H **35**
Rubens Ct. BS22: Wor 4D **12**
Ruddymead BS21: Clev 5D **4**
Rudhall Grn. BS22: Wor 4F **13**
Rugosa Dr. TA8: Berr 1A **36**
Rushmoor BS21: Clev 6A **4**
Rushmoor Gro. BS48: Back 6A **6**
Rushmoor La. BS48: Back 6A **6**
Russell Av. BS24: Lock 4G **21**
Russell Rd. BS21: Clev 4C **4**
BS24: Lock 3F **21**
Russett Cl. BS48: Back 6H **7**
Russett Gro. BS48: Nail 4C **6**
Rutland Cl. BS22: W Mare 1A **20**
Rydal Av. BS24: Lock 5D **20**
Rydal Rd. BS23: W Mare 5F **19**
Ryecroft Av. BS22: Wor 5C **12**

S

Sadbury Cl. BS22: Wor 3F **13**
Saffrons, The BS22: Wor 3F **13**
St Agnes Cl. BS48: Nail 3G **7**
St Andrews Cl. BS22: Wor 4D **12**
BS48: Nail 3G **7**
BS49: Cong 3C **14**
St Andrews Dr. BS21: Clev 5A **4**
St Andrew's Pde.
BS23: W Mare 5F **19**
St Andrews Rd. BS27: Ched ... 4H **35**
BS48: Back 6B **6**
TA8: Bur S 6B **36**
St Ann's Dr. TA8: Bur S 4A **36**
St Aubyn's Av. BS23: Uph 1D **26**
St Austell Cl. BS48: Nail 4G **7**
St Austell Rd.
BS22: W Mare 1H **19**
St Bridges Cl. BS22: Kew 1G **11**
St Christophers Ct.
BS21: Clev 2C **4**
St Christopher's Way
TA8: Bur S 3A **36**
St Clements Ct. BS21: Clev 3C **4**
BS22: Wor 5E **13**
St Congards Way
BS49: Cong 3E **15**
St David's Cl.
BS22: W Mare 5H **11**
ST GEORGES 5H **13**
St Georges Ct.
BS22: St Geo 3G **13**
St Ives Cl. BS48: Nail 3G **7**
St Ives Rd. BS23: W Mare 5G **19**
St James St. BS23: W Mare ... 2D **18**
St John's Av. BS21: Clev 4D **4**
St John's Cl. BS23: W Mare ... 6D **10**
St Johns Ct. BS26: Axb 1A **34**
St John's Rd. BS21: Clev 4D **4**
BS48: Back 6B **6**
TA8: Bur S 6B **36**
St Joseph's Rd.
BS23: W Mare 6E **11**
St Judes Ter. BS22: W Mare ... 6A **12**
St Luke's Cl. TA8: Bur S 6B **36**
St Margaret's Cl. BS48: Back ... 6A **6**
St Margarets La. BS48: Back ... 6A **6**
St Margaret's Ter.
BS23: W Mare 1D **18**
St Mark's Rd. BS22: Wor 3D **12**
TA8: Bur S 6B **36**
St Martins Ct. BS22: Wor 4C **12**
St Mary's Cl. BS24: Hut 1B **28**
St Mary's Ct. BS24: W Mare .. 1G **27**
St Mary's Gdns. BS40: L'frd ... 4H **25**
St Mary's Gro. BS48: Nail 5C **6**
St Mary's Pk. BS48: Nail 4C **6**
St Mary's Rd. BS24: Hut 1B **28**
TA8: Bur S 6B **36**
St Mary's St. BS26: Axb 1B **34**
St Matthew's Cl.
BS23: W Mare 6D **10**
St Michael's Av. BS21: Clev 6D **4**
BS22: Wor 4E **13**
St Michael's Rd. TA8: Bur S ... 6B **36**
St Nicholas Rd. BS23: Uph 1D **26**
St Paul's Rd. BS23: W Mare ... 4E **19**
TA8: Bur S 6B **36**
St Peter's Av.
BS23: W Mare 6D **10**
St Peter's Rd. TA8: Bur S 6B **36**
St Saviours Chu.
BS23: W Mare 2F **19**
Saints Ct. TA8: Bur S 1B **38**
Salcombe Gdns. BS22: Wor ... 4E **13**
Salisbury Rd.
BS22: W Mare 6A **12**
TA8: Bur S 6C **36**
Salisbury Ter.
BS23: W Mare 1D **18**
Salthouse Rd. BS21: Clev 5B **4**
Saltings Cl. BS21: Clev 5B **4**
Sandacre Res. Pk.
TA9: High 3D **38**
Sandbay Cvn. Pk.
BS22: Kew 2G **11**
Sand Bay Holiday Village
BS22: Kew 2G **11**
Sandcroft Av. BS23: Uph 1D **26**
Sand Farm La. BS22: Kew 1G **11**
SANDFORD 5A **24**
SANDFORD BATCH 1H **31**
Sandford Cl. BS21: Clev 6B **4**
Sandford Rd. BS23: W Mare ... 2F **19**
BS25: Wins 1H **31**
Sandhills Dr. TA8: Bur S 1A **36**
Sandmead Rd. BS25: Sandf ... 5A **24**
Sandpiper Dr. BS22: Wor 6D **12**
Sandringham Ct.
BS23: W Mare 4F **19**
Sandringham Rd.
BS23: W Mare 4F **19**
Sand Rd. BS22: Kew 1G **11**
Sandy Cl. TA9: High 3D **38**
Savernake Rd. BS22: Wor 4D **12**
Saville Cres. BS22: W Mare ... 1A **20**
Saville Rd. BS22: W Mare 1A **20**
Sawyers Cl. BS48: Wrax 2G **7**
Sawyers Ct. BS21: Clev 4E **5**
Saxby Cl. BS21: Clev 6B **4**
BS22: Wor 3F **13**
Saxon Ct. BS22: St Geo 4H **13**
Saxondale Av. TA8: Bur S 2A **36**
Saxon Pl. BS27: Ched 4G **35**
Saxon Rd. BS22: W Mare 1A **20**
Saxon Way BS27: Ched 5G **35**
Says La. BS40: L'frd 4G **25**
Scafell Cl. BS23: W Mare 6G **11**
Scaurs, The BS22: Wor 5D **12**
School Cl. BS29: Ban 6D **22**
School La. *BS21: Clev 4E 5*
(off Old St.)
BS25: Row 2G **33**
BS29: Ban 6D **22**
School Rd. BS40: Wrin 5C **16**
School Vw. BS48: Wrax 2H **7**
Scotch Horn Cl. BS48: Nail 2F **7**
Scotch Horn Leisure Cen. 2F **7**
Scotch Horn Way BS48: Nail 2F **7**
Scot Elm Dr. BS24: W Wick ... 6G **13**
Scots Pine Av. BS48: Nail 2F **7**
Scott Rd. BS23: W Mare 5G **19**
TA9: High 4D **38**
Scott's Hole Drove
BS27: Ched 5B **34**
Seabrook Rd.
BS22: W Mare 6B **12**
SeaQuarium 3D **18**
Searle Ct. BS21: Clev 4E **5**
Searle Cres. BS23: W Mare .. 3G **19**
Seavale Rd. BS21: Clev 3C **4**
Seaview Rd. TA8: Bur S 5A **36**
Sedgemoor Cl. BS48: Nail 4D **6**
Sedgemoor Rd.
BS23: W Mare 6F **11**
Sefton Sq. BS24: W'ton V 1E **21**
Selbourne Rd.
BS23: W Mare 5E **19**
Selwood Cl. BS22: W Mare 2A **20**
Selworthy Gdns. *BS48: Nail 3E 7*
(off Mizzymead Rd.)
Selworthy Rd.
BS23: W Mare 5F **19**
Sercombe Pk. BS21: Clev 6E **5**
Serlo Ct. BS22: Wor 3D **12**
Seven Acres, The
BS24: W'ton V 2D **20**
Severn Av. BS23: W Mare 4E **19**
Severn Gro. TA8: Bur S 2B **38**
Severn Rd. BS23: W Mare 4D **18**
Sewell Ho. BS25: Wins 3A **32**
Seymour Cl. BS21: Clev 4E **5**
BS22: Wor 3D **12**
Shadow Wlk. BS24: Elbgh 6G **21**
Shaftesbury Cl. BS48: Nail 4D **6**
Shaftesbury Rd.
BS23: W Mare 1H **19**
Shakespeare Ct.
BS23: W Mare 1F **27**

T

SAFETY CAMERA INFORMATION

PocketGPSWorld.com's CamerAlert is a self-contained speed and red light camera warning system for SatNavs and Android or Apple iOS smartphones/tablets. Visit www.cameralert.com to download.

Safety camera locations are publicised by the Safer Roads Partnership which operates them in order to encourage drivers to comply with speed limits at these sites. It is the driver's absolute responsibility to be aware of and to adhere to speed limits at all times.

By showing this safety camera information it is the intention of Geographers' A-Z Map Company Ltd. to encourage safe driving and greater awareness of speed limits and vehicle speed. Data accurate at time of printing.

Unwrap the seaweed

Finding God in the suffering

To Bel,
Best wishes
from Mark

M. S. Rixon

Unwrap the seaweed
Finding God in the suffering

ISBN 9798716959002

Table of contents

Introduction

This book has been several years in the making. The initial idea first came to me a couple of years ago when I was listening to a preacher in my local church talking about suffering. In his sermon, he mentioned the prophet Jonah and like a lot of people, I thought I knew the biblical story of how he had been swallowed by a great fish. I decided to read the Old Testament book in detail, and I realised that for God to release Jonah from the fish Jonah would have had to get rid of all the seaweed around his head. The phrase unwrap the seaweed popped up and the idea of this book was born.

The topic of suffering is a difficult one and the question "Why does God allow suffering" has been asked for thousands of years. It was clear from the start that this would be a difficult book to write, and I was also under no illusion that I would be able to give a clear answer to the question. I had however come across many people who had met and dealt with suffering in different ways, and I thought that their stories were worth telling, so I began the book.

I could not have anticipated the advent of covid-19 and the extra suffering that the disease has brought to us all. Unwrap the seaweed now seemed like a book I had to finish and so after two years or so that task is done.

I would like to thank everyone who has helped and encouraged me along the way especially Louise, Maria, Hazel, and Nigel. My special thanks to Martin Young who has allowed me to use his illustration on the book cover. Please visit his fantastic website Biblecartoons.co.uk which has many more of his wonderfully inspirational cartoons.

I also would like to thank all the Book Angels who have helped me with the final draft and with promoting the book. I have listed those who have told me they are happy to be mentioned. Apologies to anyone I have left out.

Book Angels.
J. E. Dixon
S. Walker
L. Harris
M. Hayward
C. Bryant
M. Steele
L. Rixon

Finally, a big thanks to you, because if you are reading this introduction, then there is a chance you plan to read the rest of the book.

Thank you.

Mark

Jonah's story

Jonah was a prophet. He had often answered the call of God in the past, but this time it was different. This time God was asking him to move out of his comfort zone.
“Nineveh?” said Jonah.
“You want me to go to Nineveh?”
“Yes.” replied God,
“And preach to them because of their wickedness.”
Jonah was not certain he had heard correctly.
Going to Nineveh for an Israelite was like asking a mouse to visit a cat, like asking a lamb to go to a lion or worse still like asking the blues to visit the reds.
“I really do not want to go to Nineveh.” Jonah thought.
“And it's 800 miles away. And I will have to travel by donkey. And it's going to take me forever.”
Jonah was not happy.
Now some of us in Jonah's shoes might have sat down stubbornly and simply said. “I am not going. You cannot make me.”
Jonah went one step further, or to be precise he went many steps further. He ran from Nineveh in the opposite direction. The running led Jonah to a boat which he boarded in the hope he could sail away from his problems. “Maybe,” he thought, “I will be safe at sea.”
Not so.

Ferocious storms brewed up and threatened the lives of all the sailors on board. Jonah explained that he was responsible for the storms and therefore for the threat to their lives. The sailors tried to sail to safety, but the vicious weather was too strong. It was with heavy hearts that they threw Jonah off the boat and immediately the storms stopped. You might have thought that this was the end for Jonah, but God had other plans. There was still Nineveh to preach to and Jonah was still the man for the job. Instead of drowning, Jonah was swallowed by a great fish and he spent three days languishing in the fish's belly. I guess that when you spend three days in stinking dark surroundings you find you have time to do some thinking. So here was Jonah at the depths of his life (literally) and he came to a decision. His response was to cry out to God, and this is his prayer, "' I called out to the LORD, out of my distress, and he answered me; out of the belly of Sheol I cried, and you heard my voice. For you cast me into the deep, into the heart of the seas, and the flood surrounded me; all your waves and your billows passed over me. Then I said, 'I am driven away from your sight; yet I shall again look upon your holy temple.' The waters closed in over me to take my life; the deep surrounded me weeds were wrapped about my head at the roots of the mountains. I went down to the land whose bars closed upon me forever; yet you brought up my life from the pit, O Lord my God. When my life was fainting away, I remembered the Lord, and my prayer came to you, into your holy temple. Those who pay regard to vain idols forsake their hope of steadfast love. But I with the voice of thanksgiving will sacrifice to you; what I have vowed I will pay. Salvation belongs to the Lord!'" (Jonah 2:2-9).

Sometimes we find ourselves suffering in situations where there is nothing we can do but to wait until the situation passes or learn to endure it. On other occasions, there are actions we can take to help ourselves in the situation or to prepare ourselves for a resolution. Jonah acted in anticipation of God's reply. He unwrapped the seaweed and the great fish spat him out onto the shoreline.

God once again commanded him to preach to Nineveh and this time Jonah agreed. After hearing the message that Jonah brought from God, the people of Nineveh repented of their wrongdoing and God showed them mercy by sparing them from destruction.

Section 1 The causes of suffering

1 Natural events

In 1815 people living in Indonesia (indeed around the world) were going about their business as normal. Visitors to the area would have been impressed by the sight of Tambora Mountain which stood a majestic 44,300 metres tall. The local inhabitants, however, paid little heed to the mountain as they had grown used to living under its shadow. There was a slight concern when Tambora began to tremble, and small streams of lava began trickling from the mouth. Local people began to worry but they had lived in the shadow of the mountain all their lives and so panic did not ensue, surely the volcano was safe. On 10th April, any thoughts of safety were, literally, blown apart. Tambora Mountain erupted in what is considered the most destructive volcanic event in modern history. The eruption could be heard over 1,000 miles away.

The top third of the volcano was lost as volcanic ash was thrown into the sky killing 10,000 people in the initial explosion. The lava flooded into the seas causing many tsunamis. Acrid sulfur dioxide gas spread across the world causing a global temperature drop of around three degrees Celsius. Sunlight hitting the earth was blocked by the volcanic output causing crops worldwide to fail. 80,000 people starved to death while the disease typhus ravaged its way across Europe. Economies stuttered with commodities like grain quadrupling in price. In many parts of the world, summers were turned to days of frosts and snow and 1816 was called the year without a summer.

Today the volcano is monitored for activity, but a major tremor would probably affect millions of people.

Natural events such as this, although maybe on a lesser scale, happen frequently. Every year there are some 300-400 recorded incidents. When we talk about these kinds of events our language is loaded with supposition. We describe them as being events of biblical proportion or apocalyptic (after the events in Revelations) and insurance companies use the term acts of God. Is this fair? Is God responsible for these events happening?
Indeed, many people try to blame God for these events and when they are in the middle of such events they cry out with the universal question,
"Why is this happening to me?" It's a good question and there are no easy answers.

To try and find a solution, we must watch God in action at the beginning of creation. We need to go back to Genesis, the very first book of the Bible,
"In the beginning, when God created the heavens and the earth, the earth was a formless void and darkness covered the face of the deep, while a wind from God swept over the face of the waters. Then God said, 'Let there be light'; and there was light. And God saw that the light was good; and God separated the light from the darkness. God called the light Day, and the darkness he called Night. And there was evening and there was morning, the first day." (Genesis 1:1-9).

There are a few interesting things to note here. The words clearly show that when God finished his work, he saw it was good. This begs a question regarding natural disasters. Are they good? If they are good things, then they could have been present in the original creation. If they are not good, then they must have come about later in the story. It is also interesting to note that the Bible says that the waters (and therefore the land) were gathered in one place that is there was one mass of land and one mass of water. This ties in with the scientific idea that all the lands of the earth were originally joined in one large mass called Pangaea (which is Greek for mother earth) surrounded by a super ocean called Panthalassa. Science suggests that Pangaea split into today's continents as a result of plate tectonics.

Adam and Eve were invited to look after the new earth and subdue it. Instead of following Gods commands, they disobey by eating fruit that they are told they must not eat. This deliberate act of disobedience meant that mankind's relationship with God became damaged. However, it was not just the relationship between God and man that was damaged but the whole of creation itself became broken. God's response to the disobedience was as follows,

"To Adam he said, "Because you listened to your wife and ate fruit from the tree about which I commanded you, 'You must not eat from it,'

'Cursed is the ground because of you; through painful toil you will eat food from it all the days of your life.

It will produce thorns and thistles for you and you will eat the plants of the field. By the sweat of your brow you will eat your food until you return to the ground since from it you were taken; for dust you are and to dust you will return.'"

(Genesis 3:17-19).

As a result, the world we now live in is very different from the original world. There is evidence of brokenness in all parts of creation. Natural disasters are an example of this. Other natural events that happen include disease. Illness of our bodies and the existence of pathogens such as the coronavirus is part of the brokenness.

Let's consider illness first. In the original creation, illness did not exist. Humans were designed to function perfectly but once the relationship with God was broken our bodies became the subject of decay. In Genesis chapter 2 we read,

"And the Lord God commanded the man, 'You are free to

eat from any tree in the garden; but you must not eat from the tree of the knowledge of good and evil, for when you eat of it you will surely die.'" (Genesis 2:16-17).

As we have already seen, mankind broke this commandment from God and one of the consequences of this broken relationship was that man would die. This death is about the only certainty we have in this life and the decay of our bodies comes about as a result of the original fall.

Many diseases today have a genetic element. You have in virtually every one of your cells a blueprint to make an exact copy of you. This blueprint is in the form of the molecule DNA. Imagine jumping into a Star Wars-style spaceship and travelling from one side of our solar system to the other. Now turn around and make the journey past all the planets back to where you started. If you stretched out the DNA in all your cells it would cover the distance you had travelled.

This remarkable molecule copies itself when cells divide and this process happens in your body nearly two trillion times in 24 hours, (that's a million, million times a day). When we were created this process would have been error-free. (DNA has its own self-checking process) As a result of the fall, however, the replication process can go wrong and the errors that result are known as mutations. Most of these mutations have little or no effect on the human body. Unfortunately, now and again a mutation occurs which can cause an illness. These genetic diseases range from illnesses such as Alzheimer's to many cancers. One of the saddest things I ever heard was someone being told that their cancer was a result of their personal sin. It was not. It is a consequence of the original sin of mankind.

Some diseases we have are caused by microbes such as bacteria and viruses. We are acutely aware of the problems caused by the virus Covid-19. Where do these micro-organisms come from?

First, there is the mistaken idea that all bacteria cause disease. Many bacteria are useful to us and there are some that we use for our own purposes. Without bacteria, there would be no cheese for example. It is tiny microbes that change the protein in milk into a solid form which then leads to the cheese that we eat. Microbes also play a vital part in the recycling of nutrients. Microbes, like bacteria, cause the decay of dead organisms and as these organisms begin to decay, the nutrients inside them are made available once more. Without this decay process, the earth's nutrients would get locked up in dead organisms, and life as we know it would struggle to continue. Your body also has many bacteria associated with it that have a useful function. It is estimated that the average human is carrying about four lbs. of bacteria. This is about three percent of your body weight but because bacteria cells are so much smaller than ours there are around 10 bacteria cells for every human cell in your body. These carry out such things as helping digestion in the gut.

Scientists have so far found, and identified, around 30,000 different species of bacteria. Of these around one percent cause disease. However, experts believe that they have identified nearly all the disease-causing bacteria but that there may be several million unidentified (harmless) bacteria on the planet. This means that the actual percentage of disease-causing organisms is tiny. Nonetheless, the few bacteria that do cause disease can be devastatingly dangerous. So why do some bacteria cause disease?

In the original creation, it is likely that bacteria existed in a beneficial relationship to all the other organisms on earth. Indeed, some organisms have such a close relationship that we give that relationship a special name. We refer to it as symbiosis. One example of this is the bacteria called Rhizobium which lives in the roots of some plants such as peas and beans.

When Rhizobium enter the roots a new pink coloured nodule forms on the roots. This pink nodule requires the cooperation of both the plant and bacteria to construct it and it is different to anything the bacteria or plant could produce on its own. In this relationship, the bacteria obtain food from the plant and the plants gain by obtaining nitrogen salts made by the bacteria. Plants need nitrogen salts to grow and if these are in short supply in the soil the plant can struggle to survive. Therefore, Rhizobium obtains food from the plant and the plant obtains nitrogen salts from Rhizobium. Both party's benefit. This picture of creation is a happy one where things live for the good of each other.

However, we once again have to consider that our current world has changed from the original design. The natural laws that God put in place have been turned upside down. The relationship that some bacteria had with living things has been broken and some bacteria have changed their purpose. It is possible that as decay set into Gods created world, the genetic information of living things experienced that decay. Bacteria might have lost some of their functions which could lead to them becoming dependent on the host. Instead of being in a mutually beneficial relationship they have failed on their part of the deal and moved from having a two-way symbiotic relationship and instead have a one-way parasitic relationship where they take and give nothing in return. The bacteria now cause disease and infection. The word infection probably comes from a French word meaning contamination which itself probably originated from the Latin word infectus meaning to stain.

Once again, we see that a system that was once created to be good has been tainted by the fall, some bacteria that were once beneficial now cause disease.

However, even if we accept that bacteria, which once had a noble purpose, could become twisted and cause disease, how can we explain viruses? Surely, if, as many people believe, all viruses cause disease then how can we explain their existence? How could a world created to be a good place account for viruses like Covid-19?

If viruses were part of the original plan, then it is no surprise to find people asking:

“Why did God create viruses?” and that is a fair question to ask.

Viruses like Covid-19 are fascinating things. A typical virus consists of a piece of genetic information surrounded by a protein coat. The virus gets the genetic information into a host cell and uses the cell machinery to read the instructions on the genetic material. These instructions are for the creation of new virus particles and these can then go on to infect other cells or hosts.

While they are multiplying, viruses usually cause disease to the host.

The origin of viruses is uncertain. Even biologists cannot agree on how viruses came into being and there are several theories in existence. Some people think that viruses may once have been useful and may have transferred genetic information from one species to another which could be a mechanism for the development of organisms. Another theory is that viruses were once cells in a relationship with other cells. At some time, these relationships changed so that one of the parties (the virus) became reliant on the other.

Over a longer time, the viruses lost their ability to carry out the normal functions of living cells and became totally dependent on their host, consequently causing disease. If this is true, then viruses changing over time to become diseases would be a direct result of the fall. In the case of Covid-19, the virus underwent a mutation which resulted in it being able to infect humans. Mutations are errors that occur when genetic material copies itself. This copying is a remarkably complex self-checking mechanism but occasionally errors occur which can alter the way an organism functions. This is what scientists believe happened to Covid-19. This error means that the virus now causes disease in humans with potentially devastating effects. Mutations would have begun to appear in cells as a result of the fall and so it would be true to say that the emergence of Covid-19 as a human disease is a consequence of this. The virus was not created to behave in this way. It is a result of creation being broken.

It should also be said that some diseases are linked to human behaviour. Even if our actions don't cause diseases directly then the behaviour can increase the risk of the disease occurring. These actions include smoking, overeating and not exercising. If we were to fall ill as a result of these then it is hard to see how God could be blamed. The World Health Organization, (WHO), has stopped using the phrase Act of God for the kinds of suffering we see in this section. Instead, WHO simply refers to them as natural events.

As we have seen some of these events can be made worse by our actions. We build houses beneath potentially active volcanoes, build whole cities on fracture lines and we fail to put up adequate flood defenses. We indulge in all sorts of activities that are detrimental to our health. Why does God not stop us from doing these things? That's the subject of the next section.

2 Human decisions

WARNING

The first part of this section contains graphic descriptions of vile acts. I make no apologies for this as I wish to illustrate how inhumane humans can be. If, however, you do not wish to read this description then please skip to the next page. (The passage is printed in italics.)

In 1995 a 16-year-old girl called Kelly moved in with James, a man old enough to be her father. This would be seen by many to be an unhealthy relationship but this event pales into insignificance compared to what happened next. Over the next six months, James began to dominate and control Kelly. The young girl was prevented from leaving the house and was frequently tied up. Sometimes she was tied by her hair to radiators and on other occasions, she was tied with a noose around her neck. Kelly began to suffer other attacks and mutilations. The evil that James was capable of inflicting seemed to have no limits as he tried the effect of scissors, knives, forks, a spade, pruning shears and even a hot iron on various parts of Kelly's body. In the latter part of her life, it is believed that James gouged Kelly's eyes out and then stabbed the eye sockets to see what further pain could be inflicted. In April 1996 James walked into a police station and stated that he had accidentally killed his girlfriend. Upon examining the body, the pathologist found over 150 wounds.

James was tried and found guilty of murder. In the trial the prosecutor said "It was as if he deliberately disfigured her, causing her the utmost pain, distress and degradation ... The injuries were not the result of one sudden eruption of violence, they must have been caused over a long period [and] were so extensive and so terrible that the defendant must have deliberately and systematically tortured the girl."

Most people will agree that humans are capable of the most horrific acts. Many would ask the question.
"How can a good God allow such things to happen?"
To answer this, we must once again go back to Genesis, and look at the reason we are here in the first place.

Christians believe that God created humans for his glory. Our purpose on earth is therefore to glorify God. What does that look like in practice here on earth? One aspect of glorifying God is to acknowledge that he exists and to give him praise and worship, in other words, to love him. The word love is a strange one and has all sorts of meanings. Love is an action word. If you truly love someone then you will go out of your way to do things for them. The important thing in all of this is that to show us his love, God has given us free will. This idea is crucial to the understanding of how mankind can behave in such evil ways.

Imagine that you needed something from a shop but were unable to drive. A friend of yours could respond in several ways. They could decide to let you wait until you were next out and near the shop yourself. They could tell you that they will collect it tomorrow. Or they could decide to jump in a car and go and collect it there and then.
They have a decision to make, and this is because they have free will. The kindest act would be to do the latter, but they could also choose to act selfishly. The point is that they have a choice.

Let us imagine a different scenario in an imaginary future. In this world, cars are fully automatic. They can drive on the roads without assistance. This time you could just program the car to drive to the shop. The item could be placed inside it and it could drive back. Since the car is programmed to follow your instructions, the vehicle does not make any conscious decision as to how it will behave. It has no free will. In both instances, the result is the same. You get the item you want. However, the two ways of achieving it are very different. In the first case if your friend decides to drive out now and collect the item then this would be an act that could be described as loving-kindness. In the second case, the automatic car is not being kind or showing any kind of loving act. It is programmed to do what it is told. If God had created us as puppets with no power to make decisions, then there is no way that we could love him. Everything we did would just be automatic and we could not be blamed for our actions. God has not created us like that. Instead, he has given us free will. We can use our free will to act for good or sadly to act for evil. Because God has given us this free will, there is always a chance that we will exercise the wrong choices.

This first happened in the garden of Eden when Adam chose not to obey God. As a result, all humans are tainted with an ability to act in an undesirable way. The Bible uses the word sin for the kind of action which is disobedient to God. Some of us like to think that we are good people, and we would never do anything wrong, but according to the Bible, we are all guilty of disobeying God in one way or another,

"for all have sinned and fall short of the glory of God," (Romans 3:23).

Fortunately, Christians have a solution to this problem but that's for a later part of the book. Some sin results in more suffering than others but the action is still wrong. We can all behave in this way because we all have free will to do so. We were born with a leaning towards sin. It is with us from birth.

I remember the first time I ever went lawn green bowling. I picked up the large wooden bowl and projected the down the centre of the green towards the small white jack. I was thrilled that my bowl was bang on target and it looked like my first bowl was going to be a success. Imagine my surprise when at the last moment the bowl veered off-line and missed the jack by a good margin (in fact I think my bowl went off the green into the ditch). Had I known a bit more about bowling I would not have been surprised. Bowling balls don't run straight, they have an inbuilt bias to veer off course. As a result of the first disobedience, all humans have the same kind of inbuilt bias to veer away from good behaviour and choose to make the wrong decisions. The inbuilt bias was there from our birth. Psalm 51 tells us that we are sinful from the time we are conceived,

"Surely I was sinful at birth, sinful from the time my mother conceived me" (Psalm 51:5).

This sinful nature is the root of the behaviour that can result in hurt, anguish, disappointment, and so on. Human behaviour is responsible for lots of suffering in the world. It is the result of the decisions we make due to our possession of free will. Nearly everyone would agree that if that is true then God cannot be blamed for our decisions.

3 Spiritual evil

Some people believe that evil can enter the world as a result of a spiritual attack. Many people believe that angels exist and there is a huge industry helping people link to guardian angels. I am not going to discuss this in detail here, but I can't find anything in the Bible to suggest that we have a personal guardian angel.

Christians also believe that alongside the spiritual realm of angels there is a realm of evil beings. In the Bible, there are several incidents of these malign beings causing distress to people. The classic encounter is found in Job where the devil causes all sorts of problems. It is interesting to note that Job is described as blameless and upright and yet God allowed evil spirits to attack him. This kind of attack may happen when Christians are walking in God's path and can be a sign of testing. In fact, some people think that the closer you walk with God, the more likely you are to be attacked. Even Jesus experienced spiritual attack; for example, when he was tempted by the devil in the wilderness, which we can read about in the book of Matthew,

"Then Jesus was led by the Spirit into the wilderness to be tempted by the devil. After fasting for forty days and forty nights, he was hungry. The tempter came to him and said, "If you are the Son of God, tell these stones to become bread." Jesus answered, "It is written: 'Man shall not live on bread alone, but on every word that comes from the mouth of God.' Then the devil took him to the holy city and had him stand on the highest point of the temple. "If you are the Son of God," he said, "throw yourself down. For it is written: "'He will command his angels concerning you, and they will lift you up in their hands, so that you will not strike your foot against a stone.'"

Jesus answered him, "It is also written: 'Do not put the Lord your God to the test.'" Again, the devil took him to a very high mountain and showed him all the kingdoms of the world and their splendour. "All this I will give you," he said, "if you will bow down and worship me." Jesus said to him, "Away from me, Satan! For it is written: 'Worship the Lord your God, and serve him only.'" Then the devil left him, and angels came and attended him." (Matthew 4:1-1).

It is also possible that people who do not believe in God can be spiritually attacked. I have come across many people who have dabbled with the occult and as a result, they have been affected by spiritual attacks.

So, can we put our sufferings onto the shoulders of evil spiritual beings? I believe that it is possible that people are affected but spiritual attacks but that today these are less common than in biblical times. (This might be because our walk is not as close or because we are less able to discern these attacks.) I am therefore not going to explore this in more detail here. However, if you feel you might be under spiritual attack, you should seek advice from a member of the Christian community that you can trust.

Section 2 Why God allows suffering

1 We have free will

We have free will. As we have previously mentioned this is a prerequisite for humans who are able to love God. If we don't have free will then any acts of love that we appear to do would not be acts of love but just robotic actions. One of the consequences of this free will is that we can choose to behave in an undesirable manner. This free will can result in suffering.

The free will we have been given means that we can make decisions. That means we are capable of making good decisions, but we are also capable of making bad decisions. Christians understand that there is a spiritual force that operates on earth, he is known by many names, but most people have heard him referred to as Satan. This force confuses us into using our free will to make the wrong decisions. He has no authority over God's creation. The word authority comes from the word author and we know that God is the author (creator) of this universe, (including the creator of Satan who is a fallen Angel). Satan, however, leads the rebellion against God and thinks he has authority over the system of disobedience which we see on earth from those who do not follow God. The Bible says that Satan is, "the ruler and god of this world" (John 12:31)
and it also says,
"We know that we are of God, and the whole world is in the power of the evil one" (1 John 5:19).

Satan has clear power but the authority to use it was never given to Satan. Therefore, he is using his power illegitimately, like a gun-wielding terrorist threatening to hurt people. One of Satan's most trusted weapons is that he is a liar. The Bible refers to him as the father of lies,
"..He was a murderer from the beginning, not holding to the

truth, for there is no truth in him. When he lies, he speaks his native language, for he is a liar and the father of lies." (John 8:44).

By these lies, Satan confuses us into making the wrong decisions. He makes people act in a way that leads to further brokenness of God's creation. It leads to broken relationships between fellow human beings. The result can be families torn apart, societies full of hate and ultimately acts of terrorism or full-scale war.

There are only really two choices open to us. God's way or our way. When Satan tricks us into following our desires, putting ourselves first instead of God then we fall into the trap of disobedience. So why does God allow this situation to continue? Why does he allow us to make the wrong choices?

It all comes back to the fact that God has given us free choice. Free choice to love him or free choice to disobey him. This is essential if we are to be anything more than robots. In the Bible, there is the story of the rich young ruler who asked Jesus what he needed to do to inherit eternal life. Jesus took the time to answer him and advised the young man that he needed to follow the commandments. The young man said that he had done all those things. Jesus then told him,

"One thing you lack: go and sell all of you possess and give to the poor, and you will have treasure in heaven; and come, follow Me." (Mark 10:21).

Now the young ruler had a choice to make. He could do what was asked and follow Jesus or he could choose to carry on with his life as it was. The rich young ruler decided to walk away and now Jesus had a choice. He could have insisted that the man followed him, or he could have given him his freedom of choice. Imagine that was you. Imagine you were forced to follow a particular person. What sort of follower would you be if you had no choice but to follow?

It was the same with the young man, for him to be a true follower he had to choose to follow. In the story Jesus let him walk away. We have the same choice to make. If there were restrictions on our choices, we would have no freedom at all. A jar of biscuits in the centre of the room with the instructions 'Do Not Touch' means that a child (or an adult) has real choices to make. If we lock the biscuit jar in a cupboard then there are no choices.

It is the choices people make that can result in suffering and because he has given us free will, God will not interfere with those choices.

2 To reveal our true feelings

When everything is going well, it is easy for us to feel confident and proud of what we have achieved. The nice car, the big house, the family with children, all of these are our successes. We pat ourselves on the back for being such a good person and for being a cut above the rest. We can boast about our achievements and feel good because we have made it. It was all us, us, us. If we are healthy, we might take pride in the fact that we have kept our bodies fit. We may even take credit for any cosmetic work we have had done because after all, we know how to look after ourselves.
In short, success can lead to a sense of over importance, a swagger and arrogance which sometimes can be overdone.

We all know the flashy businessman with his gold rings and big cars, jetting around the world to visit his big houses. OK, so such a person might be a caricature but, to some degree, we can recognise this behaviour in others. If we were perfectly honest there may be elements of this in us. Yet underneath all the boasting and bravado, there is a beating heart that might harbour dark secrets. Our true feelings are often not revealed. When we meet others, we all put on some kind of mask. We do not want others to know what we think and so we hide behind a persona that we want the world to see.

What do you think Jesus would have said if he came across such a person? Would he be impressed by cars, money and houses? I think that even those of us who have not read the Bible too much would be able to guess the answer. Jesus is not interested in the surface. Jesus is interested in what is under the mask. He is interested in your heart.

God knows us better than we know ourselves. We might have latent emotions and feelings deep in our hearts that we have never dealt with. We do not want the things of the dark revealed in the light. The weird thing is, however, that God already knows what those dark secrets are.

I love the illustration of this in the story of Jesus and the Samaritan woman at the well which can be found in chapter 4 of John's Gospel.

After talking to each other for a short while Jesus asks the woman to go and bring her husband to the well. She replies that she does not have a husband and Jesus replies with an answer that must have cut to her very core,

"..Jesus said to her, "You are right when you say you have no husband. The fact is, you have had five husbands, and the man you now have is not your husband. What you have just said is quite true." (John 4:17-18).

This opened the woman's eyes, and she declares Jesus a prophet. He goes on to declare that he is the messiah, and she leaves convinced.

Can you imagine how she must have felt? She has just met a man who has told her that he has living water to offer her. He has told her that,

"'"..Everyone who drinks this water will be thirsty again, but whoever drinks the water I give them will never thirst. Indeed, the water I give them will become in them a spring of water welling up to eternal life."'" (John 4 13-14).

The woman must have been full of excitement. She must have been desperate to tell people about what had happened and that is what she did.

Can you picture her running up to everyone in the town who would listen, pulling on the hem of their garments or stopping them in the streets?

"Come," she told them.

"See a man who told me everything I ever did."

Make no mistake God knows everything there is about you. He created you and knew you even while you were in the womb. He knows your innermost thoughts and feelings and sometimes it takes a difficult situation for us to face up to how we really feel.

Suffering allows us to understand the feelings in our hearts. Our masks fall off and we can be the person God wants us to be. Once we acknowledge the true feelings we have, then God can start to work on them. Precious metals need to be put into a hot fire to refine them before they are of any use. God does the same with us.

In Psalm 66 we read,

"For you, O God, have tested us; you have tried us as silver is tried." (Psalm 66:10).

While Proverbs 15 tells us,

"Take away the dross from the silver, and the smith has material for a vessel." (Proverbs 15:44).

Whether as a potter or a metal smith, God wants to shape us into the person he has planned us to be.

Once the wrong thoughts and feelings in our lives are removed, God can use us for his purpose. Without suffering we might never face up to the truth of our true feelings. To the hidden things in the heart which may be holding us back from moving into a deeper relationship with God.

If our hearts have the hatefulness of sin in them then we might respond by saying that God cannot exist.

In others, the grace of God will shine through and make our faith in God even stronger.

3 It draws us closer to God

Some of us think that God does not exist. Others think there may be a god, but they are unsure. Others still have found God and entered into a deep relationship with him. No matter which category you are in one of the things that suffering can do is make us question what is happening to us and this can sometimes lead us into seeking a deeper understanding of God.

God sometimes allows suffering so that we can realize how much we need him. In times of suffering, the experience can bring us closer to God as we seek answers to make sense of what is happening.

My local church has around 100 or so regular attendees on a Sunday morning. The One Church in Dover is quite outlooking, and before lockdown, members of the church spent time reaching out to others and inviting them to church. Many churches have done the same. They have put in place outreach programs, special musical events, tailored Christmas services, and special courses like Alpha for those with questions about Christianity. All of these have been structured to draw in people from the local community and to move them closer to God, to a point where they might commit to following Jesus. All these things are worthy endeavours and churches should not stop doing them, but during the coronavirus lockdown, an interesting thing happened. Many churches responded to the restrictions by going online with their services.

Now, you might think that if people thought the church irrelevant to them before lockdown, then they would have the same view during it. Why would they bother clicking online to watch something that they previously did not seem interested in? And yet an amazing thing happened. People began watching the service. The numbers were surprising with many people tuning in. One service recorded over 1,000 views and it wasn't just the Dover church that experienced this. Other local churches reported similar experiences. Fr Jeff Cridland, a priest at St Paul's Dover said: "We have averaged 120 people each day since we went 'live' on Sunday, March 29, from 50 countries worldwide." Canterbury Cathedral's Easter service was watched by over 10,000 people. Greg Bridges, the then chairman of the interdenominational organization Christians Together in Dover said: "I've been so delighted by the way the churches are responding to this current need with coronavirus."

But why are so many responding to the church's online services? It is because in time of suffering people often fall on their knees in prayer, often to a God that they have previously said they do not believe in. God may allow this suffering to allow us to draw closer to him. Greg Bridges said that he believes that the online services would give an "unprecedented opportunity to touch the lives of the people in Dover with a message of hope."

There are many examples of individuals in dire need turning to God. Jonathan Aitken is a good example. In 1999 Jonathan had it good. he was a conservative party member, he was in the cabinet, he owned a mansion (where he had entertained Richard Nixon), was happily married and he had his ambitious eyes on the very top job. Jonathan Aitken wanted to be Prime Minister. Not everyone shared in his success, however, and one morning he woke to find that newspapers had printed a slurry of allegations about his business deals with Arabs. They claimed he had been involved in dodgy arms deals which had netted him money. One piece of evidence was a story claiming that a stay at The Ritz had been funded by Saudi connections. This allegation, if true, would have been enough to bring Jonathan Aitken down. He immediately tried to sue the press and in court, he claimed that he had paid the bill himself, implicating his wife and daughter in the story. It was a total lie and later when the truth emerged Aitken was charged with perjury. He was found guilty.

Mr Justice Scott Baker spoke to the convicted prisoner and said, "For nearly four years you wove a web of deceit in which you entangled yourself and from which there was no way out unless you were prepared to come clean and tell the truth. Unfortunately, you were not." Jonathan Aitken was sentenced to 18 months in jail.

All that Jonathan had built came tumbling to the ground. The biblical story of the wise man building his house on the rock rather than sand comes to mind. When the storms arrived, the house on the sand crumbled into dusty rubble. Everything that had been considered important was washed away like bubbles blowing in the wind and popping open. Aitken must have felt like this on his first night in prison. He thought he had it all. He knew he had lost it all.

It is in moments like these that we start to question the values we place on the things around us. It is moments like these that we can think about our priorities. It is in desolate moments like these that we turn to God. Aitken found himself in exactly this situation. His house of cards was in ruins and he cried out to the only thing in his life that remained a constant. He cried out to God. He had in his possession a small book of Psalms and while he sat in his prison cell, he began reading Psalm 130 to himself,
"Out of the depths I cry to you, Lord; Lord, hear my voice. Let your ears be attentive to my cry for mercy." (Psalm 130:1-2).

In his book Porridge and Passion, Jonathan wrote, "a warm wave of reassurance flooded over me. Suddenly I realized that I was not as scared, helpless or vulnerable as I had thought. The author of the Psalm had been there before me."

Jonathan realized at that moment that he was not alone. He realised that he needed to draw closer to God and seek forgiveness and he understood that the path to restoring a relationship with God can be a long journey. Jonathan also realised that the journey had begun.

In 2018 Jonathan was ordained as a minister and he is a chaplain at Pentonville Prison. Jonathan spends his time trying to help others in difficult circumstances. During the festive period of 2019, he spent all the Christmas holiday working at the prison.

His story is a remarkable example of how people can turn to God as a result of suffering. Jonathan's personal suffering in prison has drawn him closer to God and given him an ability to empathise with those inside.

God can allow suffering to draw us closer to him.

4 It shapes us

Imagine a lump of clay on a potter's wheel. It is shapeless, unformed and yet it has the potential to be any object, for example, it could be shaped into a pot. This pot could be a pot of pure beauty or it could be a pot of great use. It could of course be both or something else altogether. For the pot to take shape it must be imagined in the eyes of the potter and then fashioned through the potter's hands. The potter must have a plan for what the pot could potentially look like before any work can begin. It is the same with us. God has an individual plan for every human on the planet. He knew that plan when we were born. If we follow him, we are constantly trying to become the pot that God wants us to be. The Bible states this clearly in Jeremiah,
"For I know the plans I have for you," declares the Lord, "plans to prosper you and not to harm you, plans to give you hope and a future." (Jeremiah 29:11).
In Isaiah 64 we read,
"But now, O Lord you are our Father; we are the clay, and you are our potter; we are all the work of your hand." (Isaiah 64:8).
Our experience can shape and mould the pot of our life. God is the potter, and we are the clay. God moulds us through the incidents in our life, towards the plan he has for us. Challenges can change the way we are and with each challenge we meet and overcome, the more we look like the pot that God has in mind.

These challenges, however, can cause us to suffer. Sometimes the pain is necessary for us to move forward. Sometimes suffering removes bad habits we have and removing these habits makes us more like the person God wants us to be.

Think of a diamond. A rough diamond looks a bit like a chunk of frosty glass. Once it has been cut it has an indescribable brilliance. It is interesting to note that about

60% of the rough diamond must be removed to end with the sparkling finished product. We are like diamonds; there are parts of us that need to be removed for us to become what God wants us to be. Suffering can allow that reshaping to happen.

Every time we experience pain and suffering, we can use it to become stronger. It can shape us into a stronger better person. A person who has experienced suffering can use that experience to help another in the same situation. To fully empathise with someone who is suffering we need to have felt something of what they are going through. There are many instances of this in our world. Jonathan Aitken's story is one excellent example. I would imagine that any prisoner who knew that their prison chaplain had suffered the ignominy of being locked up would find the words of that chaplain so much more powerful than if they came from a person who could not understand their experience. That does not mean, by the way, that I am advocating that all chaplains should spend time in prison or that you cannot be an effective chaplain if you have never experienced the feelings of imprisonment. Many fantastic chaplains are dedicating their lives to love and care for people in prison, and they all do an amazing job. But in Jonathon's case, God has shaped him by his experiences. I would also be pretty sure that every chaplain, priest or pastor, whether working in prison or not, has a tale to tell of how they have undergone suffering which they now realise has allowed the potter to mould them into the people they are today.

God makes pots out of people for his purpose.

Another example is found in the story of Nicky Cruz a gang member in New York who became a Christian after listening to the evangelist David Wilkerson. I am fully aware that this is a very old story, but it is such a powerful example of God at work that I do not apologise for sharing it again here. The story of Nicky is superbly told in David's book, the Cross and the Switchblade. I will summarise it to show how God can shape people's lives. In the 1950s, New York was like a jungle. Many gangs frequently fought each other, and killings were rife. One of the most powerful gangs was the Mau Mau's and it was led by a particularly vicious young man called Nicky Cruz. As the president of the Mau Mau's Nicky Cruz stabbed at least 16 other men and was responsible for a regime of terror and aggression. In this hotbed of violence members of many gangs found themselves in court and in 1958 it was the turn of seven members of the Dragons gang who were being prosecuted. Their case was of interest to Life magazine who carried a picture of the seven gang members in one of their publications. A copy of the magazine ended up in the hands of the minister David Wilkerson, who, upon seeing the picture, was filled with compassion for the young men and made his way to the New York court to preach to them. The court, however, threw him out but not before a photo was taken and published. As a result, Wilkerson gained the reputation of the man who interrupted the street gang trial. David stayed in New York and began working on the streets with gang members and drug addicts.

In 1958 his path crossed with Nicky Cruz. Let us hear the story from Nicky's angle. In his own words, he says that he had become an animal to survive in the jungle of New York. He was vicious and was one of the most notorious gang members in New York City. He was a strong leader and believed that he was invincible but beneath that tough mask, there was also a struggling heart. In an interview,

Nicky admitted that,
"When I was alone, I was one of the most lonesome persons that you ever met."
Nicky Cruz and David Wilkerson's paths met when Cruz heard Wilkerson preaching on the streets. David told Nicky that Jesus loved him. In response, Cruz spat on the preacher and later beat him up before threatening to kill him.
David Wilkerson's response was to say,
"You could cut me in a thousand pieces and lay them out in the street and every piece would love you."

It was at the peak of his terror when Nicky discovered that David Wilkerson was running a rally. Determined to disrupt and destroy the work of the preacher, Nicky and his gang members went to the meeting. Before they had a chance to inflict the chaos they had planned, Nicky stopped short. The frightened preacher knew that Nicky Cruz had come to the meeting and he prayed to God specifically for Nicky.
"Dear God," he said, "Come down and touch Nicky's life. Let a miracle come out from the darkness. Let him know that you love him. He is here and I have to believe you can do this miracle."
The response from the gang leader was amazing.
"I wanted to cry," he said, "but the last time I cried I was eight years old."
All the pain and all of the suffering that the young man had endured throughout the 19 years of his life, now crystallized into this one moment.
Nicky came to a realisation, if he was to carry on living in the same way that he had been, then he would most probably be dead before his 20th birthday.
His response was to call out to God.
"Oh, God. I don't know if it's the truth that you love me. I don't know the difference between day and night. I don't know the difference between summer and winter. But if you

really love me then come and help me."
At that point, Nicky's heart was changed, he had become a Christian.
Nicky renounced his violent life and joined a Bible college where he met his wife. He ran the organisation called Teen Challenge and went on to set up a programme called Nickcruz outreach. He has written 18 books which have been translated into 40 languages. His story has been told in two books. The Cross and the Switchblade by David Wilkerson and Run Baby Run authored by Cruz himself.

Today he is an influential Christian and has helped thousands of others on their journey towards God. The website Nicky Cruz Outreach states,
"Decades after his salvation, Nicky Cruz continues to connect with today's people of all ages, backgrounds and denominations. Because of his background, Nicky's story is vital as it mirrors the violent headlines on today's news".
Here is a great example of how God has used the suffering in someone's life to shape and mould them into the man that God wanted them to be. It is not always easy to see the purpose of our sufferings when we are experiencing them, but God can use them to help make the pot that he wants.
Today Nicky says,
"I am now a child of the Lord."

5 To help us understand our priorities

We all worship some kind of god. Some of us would profess a strong faith in a deity, a spiritual being of some sort. In the case of Christianity, the God who created this world and who is described in the Bible. Some of you may be reading this and arguing that you do not worship a god, but there is something in all our lives that drives us forward. As Bob Dylan said in one of his famous songs, we all "Gotta serve somebody."

It may be material objects, it may be money, it may be the desire for a family with children or a big house or car. What is it that you value most in life? What do you look to for your security? What do you think will bring you happiness? There is your God.

The drive for material possessions and the idea that they will bring you all the happiness you need pervades our society. Advertisements entreat us to strive for what they offer. Big companies are excellent at psychology and they know what triggers our desires. We are bombarded with adverts telling us how much better our lives would be if we had this item or the other.

The volume of adverts we are seeing seems to be massively increasing. It is believed that 50 years ago the average person would come across around 500 adverts a day on the TV, on advertising hoardings and in newspapers. By the turn of the century research showed that the number had increased tenfold rising to around 5,000 a day. About half the people in a survey believed that the level of advertising was out of control, I wonder what they would think today as it is estimated that the average number of adverts each of us is exposed to is around the 10,000 a day mark.

It is no wonder that so many of us are lured into the ideas touted by the adverts;

Disneyland - The happiest place on earth.
EA – Challenge everything
Apple –Think different.
McDonalds – I'm loving it.
Kentucky Fried Chicken – Finger lickin' good.

Some of the best slogans draw us in so that we feel we must have the experience to have a fulfilled life. There is, however, a balance to be had here.

An unhealthy love of possessions can result in us worshipping the created rather than the creator. However, cursing material things is tantamount to cursing the world that God has created. We need to constantly check ourselves to make sure we are not falling into either trap. When things are going well, we can slip into complacency. Sometimes a dose of hardship brings things back into perspective. God might use situations to help us focus on what is important.

This doesn't just affect adults. Research from the Netherlands (1.) suggests that there is a link between TV advertising and children's materialistic desires. The researchers from the University of Amsterdam stated, "Children who were frequently exposed to television advertising developed a greater desire for advertised products than children who were less frequently exposed,"

1. Opree, Suzanna & Buijzen, Moniek & Reijmersdal, Eva & Valkenburg, Patti. (2013). Children's Advertising Exposure, Advertised Product Desire, and Materialism: A Longitudinal Study. Communication Research. 10.1177/0093650213479129.

This can be a problem for us. We are spiritual beings, but we live in a material world. It is easy for us to get caught up with the wrong ideas and allow possessions to become our driving force and our god. It blinkers us to the message that God has for us; it blinds us to the word of God.
The Bible warns us in Mark's gospel,
"but the worries of this life, the deceitfulness of wealth and the desires for other things come in and choke the word, making it unfruitful." (Mark 4:19).
Sometimes we need to see things from a new perspective, sometimes we need to be shaken up and suffering can do those things.

During the Covid-19 crisis when tens of thousands of people have died, many people have begun to think hard about their lives. People realised that they missed their loved ones. That material objects were no substitute for the emotional relationship with friends and family. Sometimes God allows suffering to do this to us. Sometimes it takes pain for us to realise what is important in life.
It is part of the Christian life that we share our earthly experiences and sharing in the pain is one way we develop as a person. Sometimes all it needs is for us to be with someone, no words no actions just a presence.

6 To help us trust God

When we meet a person we know in the street we often greet them with “How are you?” Invariably the reply that returns is “Fine thank you” We also respond “Fine thank you” when someone greets us. No matter what is happening in our lives that is the stock response. Most of the time it is a reasonable response. Yes, things are happening in our lives which we wish would go away. This is probably true for everyone; even the people who seem to be the most switched on and organized. People who claim to have it all together probably have something that still niggles at them. I believe that everyone has a monkey on their back. One of the difficulties of life is that we tend to try and deal with these problems on our own. Sometimes we can sort things out, sometimes we need other people’s help but sometimes the solution is to put our faith and trust in the higher being called God. Suffering can sometimes bring us to our knees in despair until we have no choice but to cry out to God.

Imagine you had a young child in your care. When children are very young, they often try to do things that could be harmful. Obviously, if a child went to put their hand into a hot flame we would intervene with a shout and probably physical restraint. There are some situations, however, when we might consider what would happen if we didn’t take action. If a child decided to throw ice cream on the floor, some parents would try and stop them. However, if the child does throw ice cream on the floor, they are going to learn a valuable lesson. Destroying their food means they cannot eat it. This is a good lesson to learn, and we may allow it to happen despite the fact we know that the child is going to be very unhappy and probably begin kicking and screaming. If we as non-perfect parents allow this to happen then surely a loving all caring perfect God is going to allow us to make choices that may leave us in an unhappy situation. This kind of suffering can mean that we come to the end of our tether. We don't know who to turn to. We are at our wit's end. It is in these situations that people can turn and put their trust in God.

Sometimes situations are such that we realise that our coping mechanisms are just a big sticking plaster for the hurt that is happening. It is perfectly possible that the suffering is not going to go away but the only way we can deal with it is to trust God to get us through.

In 2014 the pop star Cliff Richard saw live footage on the news of his home being raided by police. Imagine how he felt when he discovered that they were looking for evidence to support an alleged sexual assault on a child. All the money in the world, all Cliff's powerful friends could not take away the feeling that Cliff must have felt while the investigations were ongoing.

Cliff said that in the darkest moments he asked himself "How am I going to get out of this mess?" However, as a man with a strong Christian faith, he has also said, "I never felt totally lost or alone."

In June 2016 the investigating officers dropped the case and there were to be no charges made. Cliff Richard can now look back at those terrible events and says of his trust in God, "So if anything, I believe harder and more furiously now than I did before."

Suffering can allow us to draw even closer to God.

Section 3 Our response to suffering

The first thing we need to acknowledge is that suffering in this world is inevitable. We are broken people in a fractured world. Suffering is an inevitable consequence of that fact and so we should not be surprised when we walk around a corner, the proverbial ladder smashes us in the face. Have you heard people in a difficult situation say, "When I come through this, I will never be the same again." Good. That means they have grown through the suffering and began to take steps to become more like the person God has in mind for them. Another little chip has been removed from the diamond; another small shape has been put into the pot on the wheel.

So, what is the best way to deal with suffering? Well, that depends upon the situation. Sometimes there are actions we need to take to navigate the river of suffering. Other times we must float passively along with the tide of potential disaster. However, there are certain principles we can look at to help us get through the muddy waters. No matter what our response is to a situation we require the undeserved favour of God to help us. We describe this undeserved favour as grace. I have used the word GRACE as an acronym to help us explore our potential responses to God. The responses we will look at are.

Give thanks
Rely on God
Act on God's word.
Communicate with God
Embrace the suffering.

Let us look at them in turn.

1 Give thanks

When things are not going well it is easy for us to put on our grumble coats and start to moan. There is no end to the targets we can find to blame for our discomfort. Other people, the weather, your parents, the world and of course God. He gets it in the neck when bad things happen especially from people who don't fully understand his nature, which I guess is most of us. However, this response is not a good one to have. Negative feelings not only make you feel worse, but it has been shown that they can impact negatively on your health.

There is a growing body of evidence to support this idea. In a study carried out by scientists at the University of Eastern Finland, (1.) it was concluded that those who stated that they had a high level of cynicism in their lives had a higher chance of suffering from dementia even when other contributory factors were removed. When she was interviewed the lead Doctor said, "These results add to the evidence that people's view on life and personality may have an impact on their health."

Other research has shown that not being thankful can affect your chances of heart disease. In a study in Finland (2.) those who showed high levels of pessimism were later found to be much more likely to die of coronary heart disease, (CHD). This was true for both men and women. The article published in BMC public health concluded that "Pessimism seems to be a substantial risk factor for death from CHD."

1. Elisa Neuvonen, Minna Rusanen, Alina Solomon, Tiia Ngandu, Tiina Laatikainen, Hilkka Soininen, Miia Kivipelto, and Anna-Maija Tolppanen. Late-life cynical distrust, risk of incident dementia, and mortality in a population-based cohort. *Neurology*, 2014 DOI: 10.1212/WNL.0000000000000528
2. Pessimism and risk of death from coronary heart disease among middle-aged and older Finns: an eleven-year follow-up study
Pänkäläinen et al. *BMC Public Health* 2016 DOI: 10.1186/s12889-016-3764-8

Now, I am not suggesting that you should be ecstatically happy about a bad situation. I am not expecting people with an illness, for example, to be jumping off the rooftops with glee. What I am suggesting, however, is that we try and adopt a kind of joyful mindset and above all to give thanks to God. Giving thanks to God is about recognising his divine nature and the things that he has done in your life. This is an instruction found in scripture.

In Psalm 31 we are implored to,

"Give thanks to the Lord, for he is good. His love endures forever." (Psalm 31:1).

This amazing psalm is worth reading right through because every verse has the same declaration. His love endures forever. The book of Ephesians says,

"we should be always giving thanks to God the Father for everything, in the name of our Lord Jesus Christ." (Ephesians 5:20).

If we realise that we cannot blame God for the situation we are in, then we can begin to give thanks to him for all the good things that are happening in and around us.

There are many examples of people in the Bible giving thanks to God.

Since the title of this book draws its inspiration from the story of Jonah, let us look at his example. When he was at his lowest ebb, Jonah realised that he needed to ask God for his mercy to save him. In the final verse of Jonah's heartfelt plea for help we see Jonah saying,

"'But I with the voice of thanksgiving will sacrifice to you; what I have vowed I will pay. Deliverance belongs to the Lord'" (Jonah 2:9).

This is amazing. At the bottom of the sea, seemingly trapped in a hopeless situation, Jonah talks to God and gives thanks. This is an example we should all aspire to. Giving thanks in all things is a great thing to try and do.

So how can we practice thankfulness? One way is to keep a

thanks or gratitude diary. You can use an actual diary for this or even some pieces of paper. I have included an outline you could use on the next page. You can freely copy this or design your own.

Gratitude Diary

Date

Things I am thankful for today.

Family

Friends

Career

Health

Myself

Other

Every day, try to write down some things you are thankful for. You can, of course, choose your own areas to focus on, but I would recommend that you think of reasons to be thankful for yourself. This may sound selfish but if you cannot be thankful for yourself, it becomes difficult to become thankful for other things like the taste of your food, the colours in a sunrise or the beauty of a flower.

Each day, look back at the things you have said thank you for. This can be useful if you ever have days when there is nothing you can think of. Another small thing I have found useful is to make a point of saying thank you to people when they do something for you. It does not matter how small that something is, the thanks you give them can grow to have a real positive effect in both of your lives and make you both feel good. This is quite difficult if you are not seeing people such as in lockdown but even then, there may be people you can talk to online or on the phone and you can say thanks to them. Try to make your thanks meaningful and not like the "have a nice day" seen in many chain restaurants where the sentiment can come over as insincere.

Being thankful like this means that you have to think about other people. This helps you identify with them and show them empathy. A little more understanding is something that we can all benefit from in our lives.

To culture thankfulness, it is good to spend time reading the Bible. There are many verses that relate to thankfulness.

2 Rely on God

When things begin to go wrong in our lives it is interesting to see how we attempt to solve the situation. Often, we try and come up with the answer ourselves. We look at any solution that might give us a solution as we seek to alleviate the problem. This is why some adverts work so well. They identify a problem we might have and then offer a solution to solve it. Unfortunately, our efforts often don't fully deal with the problem. There is usually no quick fix. If there was then businesses like the diet industry would not exist. How many diets are there on the market which promise to solve your problems? Those of you who have ever struggled and suffered with your weight will know the answer. You have probably tried them all. The same is true for the multitude of solutions offered for other problems such as smoking, alcoholism and gambling.

Now, I am not saying that we should never try out solutions to our problems. I am not suggesting that we passively sit back and let things unfold. There are often practical things we can do in response to suffering, and we will discuss that topic in the next section. But all too often relying completely on our own resources is a road to disaster. Underneath anything we try and do, we must realise that there is only one sound foundation on which we can put our trust. We can rely on God.

Let us look back at Jonah's story and how he responded. When God called Jonah to go and preach to the Ninevites Jonah was not happy. The best response in this circumstance would have been for Jonah to trust God and to go and complete the task that God was asking him to do. Jonah however decides to deal with the situation himself and he runs in the opposite direction of where he is meant to go. He jumps on a boat in an attempt to get as far away from the problem as possible. The boat gets hit by massive storms and

Jonah, suspecting that his presence on the boat might be linked to the turbulence, jumps ship. How often have we been tempted to do a similar thing in a difficult circumstance? This does not make Jonah's life any easier as a great fish decides to have him for lunch.
For three days Jonah is stuck in the fish, entangled with seaweed. It reaches a point where Jonah realises, he has to do the one thing he should have done in the first place. He trusts in God and turns to him for help.
God responds and Jonah is spat out of the fish to complete the plan that God had from the beginning.
The suffering that Jonah underwent led him to a place of utter trust in God. Sometimes our circumstances are so awful that the only response left to us is to fall on our knees and ask God for help. We must put our trust in God. How much better is it if we can do this in the first place?

Relying on God and trusting in him is scriptural.
I find the Psalms an excellent source of encouragement and direction. Many of them were written by King David of Goliath fame. That man knew what it was to be on top of the world with God, as well as being totally out of favour. The words of the Psalms, written centuries ago, still seem to resonate with us today. Here are a few, exhorting us to trust in God.

The first one advises us to be calm and explains that we can do that if we recognise who God is.
"Be still, and know that I am God. I will be exalted among the nations; I will be exalted in the earth!" (Psalm 46:10)
Next, Psalm 28 tells us that when we trust in God, we can rely on him as our defensive armour.
"The Lord is my strength and my shield; in him my heart trusts, and I am helped; my heart exults, and with my song, I give thanks to him." (Psalm 28:7)
And finally, in Psalm 9 we read that God will not leave those who trust him. A promise we look at in the next chapter.

"And those who know your name put their trust in you, for you, O Lord, have not forsaken those who seek you." (Psalm 9:10).
The Psalms are a wonderful source of strength, encouragement and inspiration. They are worth reading at any time not just in response to suffering.

3 Act on God's word

The man in the suit had just bought two sandwiches and hurriedly stuffed one down his throat as he rushed to get somewhere important. The second sandwich was wrapped in his bag, maybe for later. As the man rushed across the street, he passed a dishevelled mass of blankets in a doorway in front of which was a sign saying.

"Please help me. Homeless." The man in the suit barely gave the hands behind the sign a glance as he heard a thin voice asking for food. As he continued on his journey the man held his sandwich tightly and looked up the heavens.

"God" he pleaded.

"Please give that man what he needs."

Ok, it is an extreme example, but there might well be times when we can ask God to solve a problem when the solution lies in an action we can take for ourselves. This is not the same as relying on your own strength to get you through suffering situations. In the previous section, we saw that we need to rely on God when we are suffering, indeed one of the reasons suffering might come is to draw us closer to God. This trust in God involves us finding out his will in the situation and then listening to God and acting on his will. The next section deals with how we communicate with God to find out what he wants us to do.

When difficult situations arise then we can respond in one of two ways. Do nothing or do something.

There is an old saying, which I think originated in Hungary, that is said when everything around you is going wrong.

"My boots are full of snow."

Now in such a situation, it may be impossible to move forward. Sometimes we must rely on God to get us out of the situation but there might also be something we need to do before God can act.

We might ask God to empty our boots and then we sit back

and wonder why nothing changes.
Sometimes we might need to be asking God to take away the snow and God may do that once we have emptied our boots. It is important to try and listen to God's voice to know how to best respond in a situation. I believe there are thousands of Christians paralysed by their personal version of snow because they are waiting for God to empty their boots. They sit there shivering and suffering, waiting and waiting for the snow to stop.

In our story of Jonah, there was a crisis moment. When Jonah was at his lowest ebb he prayed to God. God's response was to get the fish to spit Jonah onto dry land. However, before Jonah could exit the fish's stomach, I believe that he had to act. He was entangled with green slime in preparation for his release from the belly I think he needed to unwrap the seaweed. Hence the title of this book.

The lockdown situation brought about by Covid-19 has seen a move of kindness from a lot of people. It takes big situations like this for us to sometimes take stock and realise what is important. People all over the world have gone out of their way to help others. The community spirit has been strong. Helping others is one of the great ways you can deal with a situation of suffering. Thinking of others before ourselves is not only scriptural but it helps in most kinds of crisis. It should be noted that sometimes there is nothing you can or need to do. It may be that you just have to accept the situation. This can be a very hard thing to do as we all like to try and solve our problems.
We need to listen carefully to God to guide us towards the kind of actions that he requires.

4 Communicate with God

When we are in difficult circumstances we must communicate with God. There is a deep-seated desire within every one of us to cry out to a higher being. This is even true of those of you who claim not to believe in God. When a crisis, disappointment, and suffering hit and we find ourselves in the depths of despair, our natural response is often to cry out.
"God help me."
Throughout this book, we have looked at Jonah's story which is an excellent example of this response. When at the very depths of his situation he communicated with God by crying out to him.

We can communicate with God in many ways. One of these is to read the Bible. Christians believe that the Bible is a letter written by the creator to his creation. Some people believe that over time men have taken the book (or books) and altered, changed and edited the texts in such a way that what we have today is a man-made construction. Christians believe that the Bible we have today is the bible that God wants us to have and the Bible itself makes claims about itself. 2 Timothy states, "All Scripture is God-breathed and is useful for teaching, rebuking, correcting and training in righteousness." (2 Timothy 3:16).
Who is correct? Can we believe the Bible and read it to communicate with God?

Before I became a Christian, I spent a lot of time reading the Bible. My parents brought me up in the Anglican church and by the age of 16, I was helping in services by serving the bread and wine. As a regular Sunday school attendee, I had read and knew a lot of Bible scriptures.

Looking back, however, I realise that I knew those scriptures in my head but did not truly understand them in my heart. I know that at this time although I was going to church, I had no real relationship with Jesus. I was not a Christian. It took me until my early twenties before I found myself asking Jesus into my life and I became born again. The amazing thing is that once I had become a Christian I returned to the scriptures and amazingly I began to see things that I had not seen before. Even today I can read a very familiar scripture, which I think I know and have studied to death and God will reveal something new, fresh and exciting. I am not saying that people without faith cannot get something out of the Bible. No matter what you believe I think that one way to deal with a crisis is to spend time talking to God and the Bible is one way to do this. God can speak to non-Christians through the Bible. He can and he does. This is fully understood by organizations like the Gideons UK (who are now known as Good News For Everyone) who spend a lot of time making the Bible available to everyone.

The Bible is a powerful book, probably the most powerful book in the world. This is why it is consistently the bestselling book in the charts. We should spend time reading the Bible as a matter of routine, but when we are suffering, the Bible can give us extra comfort.

Another way to communicate with God is through prayer. Again, it seems that a natural response during suffering is to call out to God in prayer. Prayer is important for many reasons; it helps us to talk to God and tell him how we think and feel. Prayer is not one-way communication. When we pray, we do not need to feel we have to fill every second of silence with our voice. Imagine a phone call where you were the person speaking for the whole call. You could hardly say that you have had a conversation with the other person. Listening is part of communication and a vital part of prayer. The lockdown situation has seen a massive increase in the number of online meetings taking place. Lots of people are discovering that online meetings tend to lead to people speaking one at a time and others listening while one person talks. The number of face-to-face meetings I have been in where a side meeting breaks out and trying to keep everyone focused is like holding waves back on the seashore. Often there is one person who dominates the meeting, and it can be a struggle to get the proverbial word in edgeways. Now the chairperson of an online meeting can hit the mute button. The result has been more listening and less talking. Some companies have seen the benefits of online meetings and plan to increase their use in the future. Prayer is the same. We need to talk and listen during our times of talking to God.

Some people claim that prayer does not work. This view can sometimes come from a misunderstanding of what prayer is. Some believe that prayer is like a shopping list. Ask and you will receive being an unbreakable rule. Then when they ask for something and don't get it, they conclude that prayer doesn't work. They are right. At least in their belief that the kind of prayer they are thinking of does not work.

Imagine this scenario. J the farmer (I am not going to specify gender here) wants it to rain. They have planted a good crop that desperately needs water.
"God" they call out "please make it rain."
T on the other hand has been working away from his home for several months. Upon returning T desperately wants a day out with the family.
"Please God" T prayers "give me a sunny day."
These two things cannot happen at the same time. There is much more to prayer than a spiritual wish list to be fulfilled by a benevolent father. God can answer prayers like this but when we ask God for something our requests need to be firmly in line with Gods will. The Bible tells us that,
"This is the confidence we have in approaching God: that if we ask anything according to his will, he hears us."

(1 John 5:14)

Communicating with God is not limited to Bible reading or prayer. God can talk to us in all sorts of ways. From the quiet voice inside when we are still to visions or dreams. Many people experience all of these things while others never hear God in these ways. The important thing is that we listen carefully so that we can hear God talking to us. If we believe we know what God is saying to us, then we should test our beliefs against scripture and if possible, we can talk to other Christians who may well confirm God's word to us. In my experience, if God is saying something to me then the confirmation will come in more than one way. Maybe a line from a song, possibly a scripture verse I read, and sometimes another Christian will give me a confirmation. When God speaks to us all these things will line up together and deep inside, we will be sure of what God has said. Once we know what God is saying we probably need to act.

5 Embrace the suffering

Suffering is an inevitable part of life on earth. You are a spiritual being living in a broken world and you can expect suffering to happen. Although you can try and avoid it as much as you want it will happen to you. The key is to embrace suffering when it happens.

The Bible not only supports the idea that suffering will happen,

"I have told you these things, so that in me you may have peace. In this world, you will have trouble. But take heart! I have overcome the world." (John 16:33)

There is even an indication, in the second book of Timothy, that suffering in the world might get worse,

"But mark this: There will be terrible times in the last days." (2 Tim 3:1).

And then later in the same book,

"while evildoers and impostors will go from bad to worse, deceiving and being deceived." (2 Tim 3:13).

Many people's response to suffering is to try and avoid it. Now I am not saying we should not try to safeguard ourselves against bad things happening but there is a limit to what you can do. It is stupidity to run across a road without looking, basing your action on the idea that suffering is going to happen whatever you do. In the same way, we are asked by scripture to look after our bodies. Not taking any care over our health at all and allowing our bodies to become ill is a poor tactic. However, some try and cotton wool everything about their lives. They wrap themselves in a cocoon and hope to avoid all disasters. They are behaving in a futile manner. Suffering will come in one form or another no matter how much we try to be an island. The trick is to embrace it.

Once suffering does come many people try to cope with it by trying to block out the negative feelings. Drugs are sometimes used to avoid having to face up to the suffering and to try and escape it. Both illegal drugs such as heroin and legal drugs such as alcohol have been used as coping mechanisms during crises. They give relief, otherwise people would not use them, but sadly they are not a long-term answer. They will not remove the suffering only dampen your response to it and the effects they have may then spill into other areas of life. This often leads to a downward spiral of addiction and more suffering. Even the pleasure that comes from this tactic does not last long. It is like a feather in the air. One gust of wind and the pleasure is gone. If you know of anyone who is trying to deal with things like this then they need your help and prayer. The only solution that is going to give them long term hope is to embrace the suffering and deal with it head-on.

I am not going to suggest for one moment that this is an easy thing to do. It can only be done once the person accepts that the coping solution does not work and then steps can be made to deal with the situation. One small step at a time. Here is a story of someone having this experience.

Louise was very excited. It was March 2009, and she was going on a skiing trip with the school. She loved the activity but hadn't been for a while and so had been practising on a dry slope before the holiday. On day one of the holiday, she found herself at the top of the intermediate slope. Louise launched herself and began the descent. Within a short time, things went wrong. Louise recalls the incident.

“I went around a corner and fell. I went down but the skis didn’t fall off.

I remember seeing a wall of ice coming towards me and I smashed into it. I was in immense pain, I felt sick and clammy and passed out” Louise spent the next 10 days being treated for blood clots until she was allowed to travel home. Once back in the UK, Louise went to the local hospital. A doctor looked at the injury and called for an x-ray. Soon a second doctor arrived, followed by a third and then a fourth. The doctors had never seen anything like it; the nerve in her leg had been severely damaged. It was as if someone had taken a pair of scissors and cut the nerve in two. She was told to go home and wait; nerve growth is slow (about one millimetre a month) and when she returned 18 months later the diagnosis was bad. The damage was permanent. Louise found that the damage caused immense pain. She went to see a pain specialist who diagnosed her as having Chronic Regional Pain Syndrome, (CRPS). After receiving a lot of information, Louise was started on pain medication. Medication which she still takes to this day.

The nerve damage in Louise's leg meant that her foot dropped as she walked. In an attempt to cure this, surgeons fused her ankle bones and inserted a piece of metal to keep her foot permanently at the correct angle. Later her toes began to curl, and pins were inserted to prevent this from happening. This was partially successful and as a last resort, one toe had to be amputated.

In 2019 Louise took part in a trial for a spinal cord stimulator that attempts to block some of the pain. The surgery took place but within less than a week it was clear that things were not right. The device became infected, and Louise required emergency surgery to remove the device. The operation left a wound in her back which was still recovering over a year later. Louise found her mobility was becoming worse and in consultation with the orthopaedic specialists she agreed to go forward with a below the knee amputation. This was due to take place in April 2020, but COVID-19 put a stop to that. Once lockdown finished, however, she obtained an operation date, and the amputation took place in October 2020.

Louise has now recovered from the operation and has received a prosthetic leg. She is now getting used to walking on it. All of this happened as a result of one slip on a ski slope.

Imagine that this had happened to you. What would your response be? It would be very easy to blame God for what had happened. It would be easy to give in to the pain, become a recluse, feel sorry for yourself and stay in all the time. This is not what Louise did. Instead, she has tried her best to continue with as much normal life as possible. She drives an adapted car, has a scooter and a wheelchair and, when Covid restrictions allow, she spends time out with her friend Chris. Louise has remained very positive. She still plays her guitar and hopes to get back to worshipping in the local church. She has been an active part of the prayer team doing lockdown and led online Christmas Carols for a group of ladies from the church. She is an excellent example of someone who has not allowed her situation to bring her down but instead has embraced the suffering.

She says, "Nobody wants to be in pain, I hear you say of course not. However, I was asked last year that if I could go back would I change things so that my accident never happened? My reply was definitely not, I wouldn't change things. I believe that through my accident and the journey I have taken, I have become a better version of myself. I feel that I am a kinder, far more caring person. I have time to pray for people and when one door closes another one opens. God is awesome; I have felt him with me, giving me his grace and mercies new every morning. I was always too active to pray before my accident. I used to wish and think I would love a more fluid relationship with God, praying more and building my faith. I do feel that as I am a calmer person I can and do pray more. I feel very humbled to think that the morning of my last surgery God took time to give me a Bible verse, Deuteronomy 31:8,

"The Lord himself goes before you and will be with you he will never leave you nor forsake you. Do not be afraid do not

be discouraged."
That was all the confirmation I needed. God will never leave us or forsake us. He came into the hospital with me. Even though my husband couldn't come in I didn't feel alone, not once. Because of covid-19 Mark couldn't come to see me at all, so for 10 days, I knew that God was by my side. I would honestly say that since 2009 my faith has grown. In some of my blackest and darkest moments, God has been there supporting me, alongside me. There are so many times there have been God instances, not coincidences."

It is quite clear that Louise has accepted the situation and handed it to God. As a result, she has been able to deal with the major changes in her life. Louise's story also illustrates another thing to take on board when trying to embrace hardship. Remember that you are not alone. It may help to deal with the suffering that is happening. If you have faith, then you can take comfort in the fact that Christ suffers with you,
"And surely I am with you always, to the very end of the age." (Matthew 28:20).

There will also be others suffering in the same way that you are. The church I attend merged with another church in December 2019. There were inevitable tensions as change occurred with both sides having to compromise on some of the things they did. In services, it was inevitable that people tended to talk to those that they already knew well. Changing culture, when two organisations merge, is a tricky thing. Lockdown changed that. Lockdown meant that people had to communicate in different ways. When people spoke online, the original church they were from meant little. We all realised that we were in this difficult situation together and that helped people embrace the crisis.

Finally, we should embrace the changes that occur during suffering because we need to take on board that pain can have a purpose. Imagine that you as a father are trying to teach your child to ride a bike. At first, you allow her to use stabilisers but if the long-term goal is to be achieved there will come a time when stabilisers are removed. Now comes the hard part as a parent. We can walk close to the bike and hold onto it so that it never falls, or we can let our child ride away on their own with the knowledge that they are at some time going to have the inevitable fall. We must allow the accident to happen, comfort our child and encourage them to get back on the bike. That is what God does with us in some suffering. He encourages and comforts. The suffering, in this case, has a purpose.

Suffering for someone learning to ride a bike is inevitable just as suffering for us living in this world is inevitable, and of course, bad situations can get worse. However, there is one thing we should hold onto during the suffering which should help us embrace and endure it. The story we are in is not over. The Bible suggests an ending, "And I heard a loud voice from the throne saying, 'Look! God's dwelling place is now among the people, and he will dwell with them. They will be his people, and God himself will be with them and be their God. He will wipe every tear from their eyes. There will be no more death' or mourning or crying or pain, for the old order of things has passed away.'" (Rev 21:3-4)

Section 4 God's promises to us

1 He cares for us

I read a story about a person who rang a supposed friend and got their answering service. The message read. "Sorry, I can't answer the phone right now, but I will call you after I have sorted out some of the things which are holding me back. And if I don't call, then you are one of those things."

Unfortunately, there are people in the world who don't seem to care very much about others. They carry on with their own lives wearing people-blinkers. They never seem to care about anything or anyone else. Thankfully, God is not like that.

One of the first promises that we can take on board is that God cares for us. This care is not casual caring. God has a deep desire to look out for your wellbeing. However, it is easy in the middle of suffering to think that this is not true, to believe that you are all alone. No one understands your situation. No one cares about you. You are not worth bothering about. If you look upwards at night and see the unimaginably large universe spread before you in a starry sky it is easy to see why people can feel insignificant. It is easy to think that no one could be remotely interested in one small, tiny person in the whole universe. Think again. The good news is that God is interested in the tiny details of your life because he cares for you.

You may feel small and insignificant on occasion but there are several things to remember. First, you are unique. There has never been anyone on the planet exactly like you and there will never again be anyone like you on this planet. Your DNA is unique to you and even identical twins have different likes, dislikes, and personalities. They even have different fingerprints.

Secondly, God knows you intimately and this knowledge of you began before you were even born. The Psalms express this beautifully,

"For you created my inmost being; you knit me together in my mother's womb. I praise you because I am fearfully and wonderfully made; your works are wonderful, I know that full well. My frame was not hidden from you when I was made in the secret place when I was woven together in the depths of the earth." (Psalm 139:13-15)

God created us for his glory and naturally, he cares for his creation. Although it is easy to listen to worldly ideas and see ourselves as insignificant, the Bible suggests a different reality. In Gods eyes, you are very valuable.

In Matthews's gospel, we read,

"Are not two sparrows sold for a copper coin? And not one of them falls to the ground apart from your Father's will. But the very hairs of your head are all numbered. Do not fear therefore; you are of more value than many sparrows." (Matthew 10:29-31)

Because God values your life, he cares for you.

Sometimes it can feel like God doesn't care. God may act in a way that makes us question his care for us. Our questions come because we cannot see the big picture of what God is doing in our circumstances. Christians believe that Jesus was God on earth, and we can see this apparent lack of care in Jesus life. One such example happened when Jesus was with his disciples in a boat which we can read in Mark's gospel.

"That day when evening came, he said to his disciples, "Let us go over to the other side." Leaving the crowd behind, they took him along, just as he was, in the boat. There were also other boats with him. A furious squall came up, and the waves broke over the boat, so that it was nearly swamped. Jesus was in the stern, sleeping on a cushion. The disciples woke him and said to him, "Teacher, don't you

care if we drown?"
He got up, rebuked the wind and said to the waves, "Quiet! Be still!" Then the wind died down and it was completely calm.
He said to his disciples, "Why are you so afraid? Do you still have no faith?"
They were terrified and asked each other, 'Who is this? Even the wind and the waves obey him!'" (Mark 4:35-41).
It is clear from this scripture that, far from not caring about his disciples, Jesus acted in a supernatural way to ease their concerns. Although Jesus at first appears not to care, his actions allow the disciples to learn something about their faith and Jesus' nature. When God appears not to care for us, the reason for his actions will not always be apparent. We just need to trust in his promise that he does and will care.

God's ultimate care for you was that he sent his son to earth so that you could be forgiven for your sins. John 3:16 "For God so loved the world, that he gave his only Son, that whoever believes in him should not perish but have eternal life" We will look at this in more detail in the last part of the book where we will look at God's response to us.

2 He will not leave us

The Bible is filled with God's faithful promise that he will not leave us. We find this promise in the Old Testament book of Joshua,
"I will never leave you nor forsake you." (Joshua 1:5)
We come across a similar promise in the New Testament book of Hebrews,
"For God has said, 'I will never fail you, I will never abandon you'" (Hebrews 13:5)
Jesus also made the same promise to his grieving disciples, upon his return to heaven,
"'No, I will not abandon you as orphans—I will come to you'" (John 14:18). Many people who have been in difficult situations can testify to the fact that God has not left them. A mother called Kelly tells one such story.

August 4th, 2014 began as a normal day for Kelly and her four-year-old son Jude. They were having a pleasant time visiting Grandma. The sun was shining, and the school summer holidays had begun which meant that Jude's brother Joel was looking forward to spending time playing with Jude. Suddenly Jude fell and hit a stone floor. Immediately Kelly realised that something was not right. Jude's leg was swelling rapidly, and an upset household called an ambulance. In a blaze of blue lights, Kelly accompanied Jude to the trauma unit singing to him all the time. He went for an x-ray and was screaming with the pain. The x-ray revealed a broken thigh bone and Jude was sent to the operating theatre. Jude's dad Damian arrived and being a fixer, he wanted to mend his broken son, but there was nothing he could physically do. While they were waiting for the operation to finish Kelly and Damian prayed to God.

Kelly recalls that they were expecting Jude to emerge with a plastered leg and be able to go home. Instead, the young boy's leg was in traction. The nurses explained that he would have to stay in that position for six weeks and would have to remain in the hospital for that time. Kelly was devastated. Questions poured through her mind. How could she keep a four-year-old still for six weeks? How would she be able to run her business (in the end it had to close) and how was she going to be able to occupy her other son for the duration of the summer holidays while she was in the hospital with Jude? Kelly did what many people do when their lives are catapulted upside down. She turned to God for comfort. She trusted in the words found in the Biblical book of Philippians,

"Do not be anxious about anything, but in every situation, by prayer and petition, with thanksgiving, present your requests to God. And the peace of God, which transcends all understanding, will guard your hearts and your minds in Christ Jesus." (Philippians 4: 6-7)

The following weeks were very difficult. Jude was in a ward with different patients coming in and out each day. There was no privacy, and he was not able to get much sleep. She tried playing Christian music on her phone to create a pleasant atmosphere for Jude but there were too many other people to get any peace. The August days were long and hot and while had visitors, his young friends often got bored as Jude was unable to move. One night Jude's leg began to violently tremble. "It was just like shaking a sheet out of a washing machine," Kelly recalls.

It soon became apparent that the leg was not healing, and Jude needed another operation. Kelly prayed that Jude would come through the second lot of anaesthetic and at this time she took comfort from knowing that her local church friends were praying with her. "You are alone," she said, "but knowing that the church is praying gives you so much strength." Kelly wondered how people who do not know Jesus manage to get through traumatic times.

The long days by Jude's bedside were to begin again. They were harder than before. Kelly continued praying and took solace and hope from small things like the sun rises she saw every morning. One day it was gloriously hot and out of nowhere a shower of rain came swiftly followed by a rainbow. Seeing Gods promise gave Kelly renewed encouragement. She remembers thinking “There was hope. God did not leave us. He knows the pain and suffering of Jude’s leg and the pain in my heart.”

Eventually, the time in the hospital came to an end. Jude came out of traction and needed to use a wheelchair. The young lad had to learn to walk, jump, hop, ride his bike and swim again. Kelly thanked God that the family had come through the suffering and remembers thinking “What the devil meant for harm; God will use for good.”

You might think that this story has enough suffering for one family to have to go through, but life has a nasty habit of stacking the dice against us and in 2019 another incident occurred.

This time Kelly and Jude were walking through Elham Forest with her cousin Emma and her dog. Once again, Jude fell over, and Kelly felt her heart stop. She knew instantly that there was a problem. There was no phone signal in this part of the forest, so Emma went off to try and contact an ambulance. But they seemed to be taking forever. Then a man who knew the forest well stumbled across them. He called another ambulance and gave a detailed description of exactly where in the forest they were. Kelly remembers thanking God for that man.

Once in the hospital, an exploration of the injury led the doctors to realise that there had been a cyst on the bone from the first operation. Routinely this condition is picked up by x-ray but due to the large number of x-rays Jude had undergone the first time he was in hospital, there had been no final x-ray before he left. The cyst meant that the new break was inevitable. It was going to happen eventually. Jude’s brother was angry. His father broke into tears.

The family did a lot of praying and crying together. It was hard to understand why this had happened to Jude again. Eventually, the surgeons pinned and plated his leg again and it was back into the old familiar wheelchair. This time Jude was not able to go to school and this led to anxiety as he felt out of control. Kelly found herself asking
"Why are we going through this again? Why do I have to do this on my own again? How do I get Jude out of this again?" These kinds of questions are not uncommon in these kinds of situations.

In March 2020 there were plans to take the metal out of Jude's leg before it grew over the bone. Then lockdown, due to Covid-19, hit. Jude's operation was due but now under threat. Kelly prayed and trusted God that if the operation did not take place, there was a reason. Damian went into the hospital to speak to the surgeon, but the surgeon was in the operating theatre. Later that day the receptionist rang and said that the surgeon was going to do the operation. This was a miracle because at this time letters were going out to nearly everyone who was waiting for surgery saying that their operations were being cancelled. Jude, however, went into the hospital for surgery but due to the covid-19 restrictions, Damian was not allowed in. However, Damian managed to wait outside the theatre and was given special permission to go in with Jude while the anaesthetic was being given so that he could comfort his son. This was unheard of and Kelly believes it was an example of God in action. Jude was due to stay in the hospital for recovery but the whole hospital had to close in anticipation of covid-19 patients and so he had to come home.

Jude had to spend his home recovery in lockdown. He was not able to have visitors.
Kelly says that he has dealt with it amazingly well helped by PE with Joe Wickes.

At the time of writing, Kelly says,
"Jude is making a great recovery and God is meeting our needs. God will use it for good. He already has and we trust God for the future."
Kelly can truly testify that God has been with her and the family throughout the journey.

Some people claim that God has abandoned them. They claim that God is not with them and that they feel all alone. It's a good question to ask. Does God ever leave us? I don't believe that he does. I have heard it said that God abandoned Jesus on the cross. In the last hours before his death Jesus prayed,
"About three in the afternoon Jesus cried out in a loud voice, "Eli, Eli, lema sabachthani?" (which means "My God, my God, why have you forsaken me?")." (Matthew 27:46). Theologians will tell you that Jesus was unique in being cut off from God's presence. I agree with this and believe that we are never away from it.

Sometimes, of course, we might feel God as f God is not with us. Maybe it is because, like Jonah, we are running away from God. However, even when he was on his way to Nineveh, Jonah was never out of God's presence. No matter how far away we feel God is, there is nowhere we can go that is out of his presence. Some biblical assurances should give us comfort.
"Have I not commanded you? Be strong and courageous. Do not be frightened, and do not be dismayed, for the Lord your God is with you wherever you go." (Joshua 1:9)
While in the book of the prophet Isaiah we read,
"..Do not fear, for I have redeemed you; I have summoned you by name; you are mine. When you pass through the waters, I will be with you; and when you pass through the rivers, they will not sweep over you. When you walk through the fire, you will not be burned; the flames will not set you ablaze." (Isaiah 43:1-2).

When we read words like this, we can have absolute confidence that no matter what everyone else does in a crisis, there is a God who promises to be with you, who promises to support you and who will always be there by your side.

3 He is our solid rock

When we hit a problem in life our instinct is to try and fix it if we can. We often try to take charge of the situation and look to ourselves for the solution. As we have seen in previous chapters, sometimes there are things that we need to do, there is seaweed to unwrap. Sometimes however we need to sit back and wait for God to act. This sometimes takes patience and trust. However, we can do this if we stand on another promise of God. He is a solid rock on which we can stand. He is our foundation upon which we build. If we stand on him, we can be sure of a firm footing.

The classic Bible story illustrating this is the parable of the wise and foolish builder told by Jesus in Matthew, "'Therefore, everyone who hears these words of mine and puts them into practice is like a wise man who built his house on the rock. The rain came down, the streams rose, and the winds blew and beat against that house; yet it did not fall, because it had its foundation on the rock. But everyone who hears these words of mine and does not put them into practice is like a foolish man who built his house on sand. The rain came down, the streams rose, and the winds blew and beat against that house, and it fell with a great crash.'" (Matthew7:24-27).

Imagine the two men looking at where to build their houses. The sand seems like a good place. It is easy to work with and the house can be put up quickly. The rock seems like hard work. It will take some serious digging to lay the foundations and build the house.

Once the two houses are built, they look pretty much the same. This is like looking at someone who has their faith in their own works, for example, their finances, and someone whose trust is in the rock of God. To the outside world, they might look similar although a closer inspection will reveal differences.

When the storm hits, however, the differences became very

visible. In terms of the houses, the one built on the rock withstood the battering but the one built on the sand fell with a great crash. We might see the same in the lives of the person who trusts in money and the person who trusts in God. In the long run, security belongs to the one who is standing on the rock of God.

The danger for us, in times of suffering, is to build our own towers. Those towers could be towers of money, status, or trust in material objects. People build those towers for lots of reasons. In medieval times towers were built to give people security. Knowing the tower was there was enough for peace of mind. They also built them for safety. Being able to climb inside a tower during a storm gives you a place where the storm cannot hit you. People also built towers to say, "Hey we are here" It gave the people status and put them on the map. The problem with these towers that we build ourselves is that they do not always live up to the promise of security. They cannot be relied upon. Money can be lost, and it cannot buy everything. Your reputation can be blown aside with one comment and your material objects begin decaying from the time you buy them. The only trustworthy, eternal foundation in which we need to trust is the rock of God. In the Old Testament book of Proverbs, it says,

"The name of the Lord is a fortified tower; the righteous run to it and are safe." (Proverbs 18:10).

I love this verse. Not only is the name of the Lord a tower but it is fortified. That means it is strengthened to withstand everything that can be thrown at it.

We can put our trust in this tower because God has promised it.

Many people find the words of the Psalms can be a wonderful source of comfort and reassurance that God is our rock. The following verses are good examples.

"The Lord is my rock, my fortress and my deliverer;
my God is my rock, in whom I take refuge, my shield and the horn of my salvation, my stronghold." (Psalm 18:2).

"Truly he is my rock and my salvation; he is my fortress, I will never be shaken." (Psalm 62:2).

"Be my rock of refuge, to which I can always go;
give the command to save me, for you are my rock and my fortress." (Psalm 71:3).

4 He gives us an answer to our mortality

There are lots of different ideas about how life on earth has arrived on its journey through time to its current position. Many people believe that the highs and lows we experience as part of this life are chance events, that there is no driving force behind it, like throwing a set of dice and seeing how they land. This view can make us feel small and inferior, without a purpose. Some people however look at the whole universe; the stars, the planets, the oceans and deserts of the earth and they look at living things, at human beings and they wonder at the apparent design of it all. They look at human beings and say to themselves. I believe I can see a purpose in the things that happen; I believe I can see an intelligence behind our design. Christians believe that this intelligence is the creator God of the Bible.

A God who put the whole thing in motion, who lives with us through both triumphs and sufferings and a God who knows exactly how the plan will end and who knows every part of his creation intimately and lovingly. That includes you. The Bible says that God loves you very much.
"Because of the Lord's great love, we are not consumed, for his compassions never fail." (Lamentation 3:22).
I believe that God not only made you but knew about you before you were even conceived. He knows everything there is to know about you, your life is in God's hands and as we have read earlier, the Bible says he cares for you very much. That makes you very special. You are also unique.

When you look in the mirror you are looking at the only version of you that exists. No one will ever go through the exact same highs and lows as you. This life is not a practice run and it is up to you to live that life in the best way that you can. One of the things suffering can do is to make us aware that we are mortal beings. It can make us realise how small we are and how big God is. This ultimately can cause us to consider our own mortality.

If you are already a Christian, then you can take comfort in your suffering by relying on God and standing on his promises. God never says he will take away our suffering on earth, but he has given us the ability to cope with it. If you have faith and need help to deal with the situation you are in, then please make contact with other people of faith that you know and trust. Your local church should have people who can pray for you.

If you don't have a relationship with Jesus, then I would like to commend you for reading this far. The final part of this book will explain how you can enter such a relationship and become a Christian. You might feel that you are not ready yet. However, it may be that God has been working on you for some time. It might be that things you have read, things you have heard and even things you have seen on the TV or the internet have led you to this place and time. Some of you might feel that the whole of your life has led to this one specific moment. If so, then please read on.

Final thoughts

We have discussed in this book why God created you? It was so that you could have a relationship with Him. The problem is that although God made us, we are also broken. The Bible says that all humans do things wrong and fall short of God's expectations,

"for all have sinned and fall short of the glory of God." (Romans 3:23).

The good news is that God is in the business of fixing broken people and he has a plan for your life. That plan came in the form of God's son Jesus. When Jesus died on the cross, he opened the way for you to have a relationship with God. This is Gods ultimate promise to us.

By confessing our sinful nature and trusting in Jesus we enter that relationship, and the Bible says we become born again.

God wonderfully made you.

He knew you before you were born.

He promises to be with you in your suffering and he has a plan for your life.

He loves your uniqueness so much that he sent his son to die on a cross for you personally so that you could enter a relationship with him and be part of his plan.

So, after reading this book you should be able to look in the mirror and say:

"God has promised that if I follow him, he will help me through all my suffering."

The question then is: "How will you respond?"

If you are sorry for the way you have been living and want to enter into a relationship with God, then you could open your heart to Him and respond with the following prayer.

Dear God,
I know I am a broken person and I need you in my life.
I am sorry for the ways I have lived my life without you.
I know that you will be with me in my suffering and that you promise to never leave me. I know that I am wonderfully made and that you love me so much that you sent Jesus to die on the cross so that my relationship with you could be fixed. You are the solid rock on which I wish to stand.
I repent of my sins and ask Jesus into my life to be my Lord and Savior.
Amen.

If you have said this prayer with meaning, then the Bible says you have been born again.
One of the first things you could do is to contact your local church and talk to them about what has happened.
There you will meet other believers and they will be able to answer any questions you have.

About the author

Mark was born in South Wales, but he has lived and worked in Dover for over 30 years. He is a biology teacher at The Duke of York's Royal Military School, a boarding school set in 150 acres of land. Mark loves walking, photography, playing bridge, reading and writing. He is a keen advocate of the Duke of Edinburgh's award of which he is an assessor. Mark is a member of Bernard Magee Bridge (BMB), a company that runs seminars, online events, bridge holidays and cruises.
He has a strong faith and attends The One church in Dover. He is married to Louise and has one daughter.

Weblinks.

The Duke of York's Royal Military School.
WWW.doyrms.com

The Duke of Edinburgh award.
WWW.DofE.org

BMB
WWW.bernardmageebridge.com

The One Church Dover.
WWW.onechurchdover.org

Printed in Great Britain
by Amazon

78390977R10046